EXPLORING PLANET EARTH

JOHN HUDSON TINER

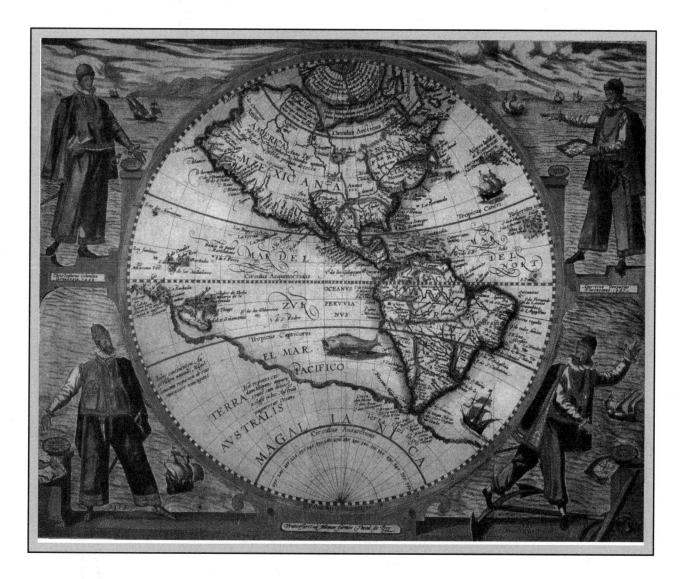

Master Books

EXPLORING PLANET EARTH

First printing: September 1997
Sixth printing: May 2007

ISBN-13: 978-0-89051-178-7
ISBN-10: 0-89051-178-0
Library of Congress Control Number: 97-70171

Photo credits for page 132: Library of Congress

Printed in the United States of America.

Please visit our website for other great titles: www.masterbooks.net

For information regarding author interviews, please contact the publicity department at (870) 438-5288.

Dedication
This book is dedicated to LaMar and Janice Marshall

This compass is a replica of the one used by Christopher Columbus on his first voyage across the Atlantic Ocean.

Table of Contents

Sextant

CHAPTER 1

HOW BIG IS THE EARTH?

Map dating from 1660

People throughout the ages have felt the urge to explore beyond the horizon. What wonders lay across the wide expanse of the ocean? What mysteries waited on the other side of the mountains?

Important discoveries have been made by professional explorers, dedicated scientists, talented amateurs, and ordinary people who became seekers after adventure. Their discoveries are interesting and exciting. Just as dramatic are the stories of how the discoveries came to be made.

Exploration takes many forms. It is not merely the quest for new lands, but the quest for knowledge about the earth. The earth does not give up its secrets easily. Exploration alone is not enough. Research in the laboratory plays a part, too. In this book we'll look at the most exciting examples of each kind of discovery.

The quest for adventure began with a simple question. What is the shape and size of the earth?

Eratosthenes (er-uh-TAS-theh-neez) grew up in a town on the coast of Libya in northern Africa. He lived about 250 years before the birth of Christ, more than two thousand years ago. He studied at Alexandria in Egypt and at Athens in Greece. He traveled widely. He studied and wrote on mathematics, astronomy, and geography. He gained fame as Greece's most talented scholar.

Although born and raised in Africa, Eratosthenes was a Greek.

The cities of northern Africa became Greek following their conquest by the greatest general of ancient times, Alexander the Great. This famous general lived almost 350 years before the birth of Christ and well before the Roman Empire. Alexander the Great conquered Egypt, parts of Europe, and Asia as far east as India. He died of a fever in Babylon at age 32.

Upon the death of Alexander the Great, his conquest was divided among four Greek generals. Ptolemy III (TOL-uh-mee, the "P" is silent), a descendent of one of these generals, ruled northern Africa. This kingdom included part of Egypt and the city of Alexandria.

In Alexandria, Ptolemy opened a library and museum. He ordered a search of all ships, caravans, and visitors who entered his realm. When Ptolemy's men found books, maps, or interesting documents, they sent the documents to the library to be copied.

Ptolemy chose Eratosthenes to take charge of the library. Eratosthenes threw himself into the task. The library at Alexandria became a storehouse of the vast knowledge of the ancient world. Scientists came from all over Greece to study there.

Ancient Greeks discussing their different ideas about the earth.

Eratosthenes made many exciting discoveries. But his most astonishing achievement was calculating the distance around the earth. He did this at a time when many of the more backward and superstitious people still believed the earth to be flat.

The ancient Greeks understood that the earth was a sphere; that is, a ball. This was clear from several observations. The best argument for a spherical earth occurred during a lunar eclipse. The shadow of the earth as it fell on the moon was circular in outline.

Other observations pointed to a spherical earth, too. For example, as a ship sails out to sea, the hull of the ship disappears from view first. The masts disappear last. If the earth were flat, the ship would grow smaller as the distance from shore increased. It would be hidden from view by haze in the atmosphere, but it would not disappear below the horizon as it does on a curved earth.

In addition, travelers to the north reported that the North Star rode higher in the sky. On the other hand, travelers to the south said the North Star circled closer to the horizon.

None of the Greeks ever traveled to the North Pole or to the equator. They believed the North Pole to be eternally frozen and far colder than a human being could endure. Nor did the Greeks ever travel as far south as the equator. They believed scorching sands of a worldwide desert circled the earth at the equator. Explorers foolish enough to travel there faced certain death.

But if an explorer could go to the North Pole or to the equator, the Greeks knew what he would see in the night sky. At the North Pole the North Star would be directly

Moon's Orbit

The ancient Greeks knew the earth was a sphere because of the shadow it cast on the moon during a lunar eclipse.

overhead. At the equator, the North Star would skim right along the horizon. South of the equator, the North Star would disappear entirely. This changing position of the North Star is best explained by the earth being spherical.

Eratosthenes agreed with the other Greeks that the earth was spherical.

Very well, Eratosthenes wondered, *how big is the earth?* If a person set out in one direction and traveled until he returned to his starting point, how far would he travel? No one knew. Without actually making the journey, how could a person find the distance around the earth?

The answer came to Eratosthenes as he read about a deep water well in Syene (now Aswan) in southern Egypt. On June 21, the longest day of the year, the sun is at its highest position. Each year at noon on that day in Syene, the sun's rays reflected from the water at the bottom of the deep well. The sun had to be exactly overhead.

At the same hour on the first day of summer in Alexandria, the sun never becomes exactly overhead. Tall buildings cast small shadows.

The sun does not precisely repeat its path every day. During winter the sun's path takes it lower in the south. Its rays are more slanted. During summer the sun's path carries it higher to the north. Its rays are more directly overhead. (The changing path of the sun is actually due to the tilt of the earth's axis, not a change in the sun's position.)

Imagine this experiment. Eratosthenes goes out at noon each day and measures the shadow of a nearby tall building. The length of the shadow doesn't change much from one day to the next. But from month to month it becomes clear that the shadow isn't always the same length, even at noon. During winter, the shadow is long and points north at noon. During summer, the shadow points north, too, but it is much shorter.

The sun's rays are more direct during summer. This warms the earth's surface. The sun's rays are more slanted during winter. Sunlight is spread out over a greater area

and doesn't warm the earth's surface as much.

Why did the sun shine directly overhead in Syene on the first day of summer, but not in Alexandria? In fact, the sun never reached directly overhead in Alexandria. Why?

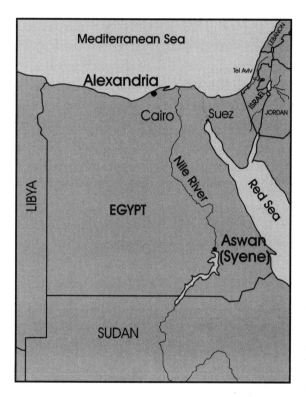

The distance between Syene and Alexandria is 1/50th of the distance around the earth.

Then Eratosthenes figured out the answer. Syene was directly south of Alexandria. This difference in position of the sun, Eratosthenes reasoned, could only be due to the curve of the earth's surface from Syene to Alexandria.

The Greeks measured angles by dividing a circle into 360 equal parts. Each part is a degree. Point straight out at the horizon and then bring your arm directly overhead. Your hand has traced out an angle of 90 degrees.

The length of the shadows showed that the sun was seven degrees south of the overhead point in Alexandria. Seven degrees is about 1/50th of a complete circle. Therefore, the north-south distance from Syene to Alexandria is 1/50th of the total distance around the earth.

Eratosthenes could calculate the distance around the earth by measuring the distance from Alexandria to Syene and multiplying this distance by 50.

What was the distance between the two cities? His calculations would be no better than his knowledge of their distance. He checked the maps of his day, but the maps were much too crude and inaccurate to be of help.

Eratosthenes questioned professional runners who carried messages from town to town. Their routes had been established for hundreds of years. These professional runners set the distance between the two cities at 5,000 stadia.

Eratosthenes wasn't satisfied. He asked for the help of the military. A general instructed his soldiers to march off the distance between the cities. They, too, arrived at a distance of 5,000 stadia.

Eratosthenes carried through with the calculations. He reached the conclusion that the earth's circumference is 250,000 stadia. We're not certain today the length of a stadia. We think it is the distance of an event in the Greek athletic games, the distance a sprinter could run without getting out of breath. Using the best value for the stadia that we have, Eratosthenes' distance around the earth works out to be about 24,540 miles. The accepted value is 24,875 miles, a difference of

only 335 miles. So he was very accurate, indeed.

Eratosthenes said, "If the great distance were not an obstacle, we might easily pass by sea from Spain to India!" This idea went unheeded until 1492 when Columbus began such a voyage.

Eratosthenes' result was so good that in modern times scientists refused to believe it. How could an ancient Greek use a water well to determine the earth's size? Preposterous! It seemed almost improper for Eratosthenes to be so accurate. He had no business being so good!

Other Greeks refused to accept the figure for an entirely different reason. Eratosthenes made the earth a much larger place than the Greeks had imagined, and it made the known world too small in comparison. It made Greece a tiny country in a vast, unexplored world. They rejected Eratosthenes' value in favor of a smaller, incorrect one.

Today, however, we know that he succeeded to an amazing degree. Eratosthenes is known as the man who measured the earth.

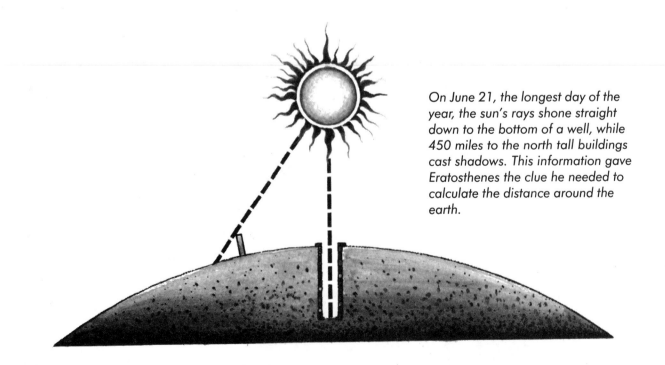

On June 21, the longest day of the year, the sun's rays shone straight down to the bottom of a well, while 450 miles to the north tall buildings cast shadows. This information gave Eratosthenes the clue he needed to calculate the distance around the earth.

Questions

How Big Is the Earth?

*Choose **A** or **B** to complete the sentence.*

1. Exploration is a quest for
   - A. knowledge about the earth.
   - B. new lands.

2. Alexandria was a Greek city, but located in
   - A. the Arctic.
   - B. Egypt.

3. Alexandria had
   - A. the greatest library of the ancient world.
   - B. the world's deepest well.

4. Eratosthenes needed to know the distance from Syene to Alexandria to
   - A. prove the earth is round.
   - B. calculate the distance around the earth.

5. Some ancient Greeks refused to accept Eratosthenes' measure of the size of the earth because it made the earth seem too
   - A. large.
   - B. small.

Thought questions:

6. Is intelligence the same as knowledge?

_____

_____

7. Do you think ancient people were as intelligent as people of today?

_____

_____

8. In what way can it be said that Eratosthenes explored the earth?

_____

_____

CHAPTER 2

MASTERS OF THE MEDITERRANEAN

The Phoenicians were the greatest navigators and explorers of the ancient world. They ventured into regions where no one else dared to go.

The brave Phoenicians lived all along the southern and southeastern shores of the Mediterranean Sea. Two of their ports are Tyre and Sidon, mentioned in the Bible. Homer wrote about them in his famous poems. The Phoenicians were a sea power more than a thousand years before Alexander the Great. The Phoenician ports eventually fell to Roman conquest. By the time of Jesus they had faded from the world scene.

The Phoenicians navigated by common sense and the sun and stars. The sun guided them by day. At night they checked direction against star constellations like the Big Dipper.

The Big Dipper, along with some nearby dimmer stars, make up a constellation known today as *Ursa Major*. The name means "big bear." The figure has not changed in thousands of years. Shepherds and sailors of ancient times saw the same arrangement we see today. Of course not everybody gave the distinctive pattern the same name.

The Big Dipper was important to all who sailed the seas.

The first mention of the Great Bear is found in the Bible in the Book of Job. The Lord asks, "Can you guide the Great Bear with its cubs?" (Job 38:32). The Hebrew shepherds imagined that the bowl of the Big Dipper formed a bear. The three stars of the handle were three cubs following along behind the Great Bear.

The two bright stars at the front of the dipper point to Polaris, or the Pole Star. The Phoenicians were the first to recognize the importance of the Pole Star in guiding them. Today, Polaris is less than one degree from celestial north pole. However, the earth wobbles on its axis. A complete wobble would take 25,800 years. At the time of the

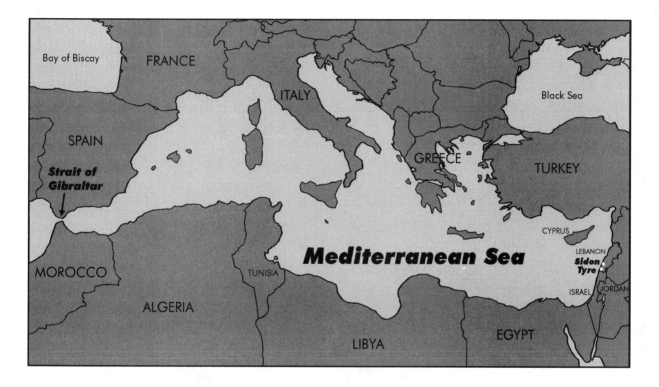

From their home ports of Tyre and Sidon the Phoenicians sailed to and controlled most of the Mediterranean.

The ancient Phoenician sailors pictured the Great Bear as a sky chariot. To travel west, they sailed with the sky chariot to the starboard, or right side, of their vessel. Not only did the sky chariot show the direction to north, its height gave some hint as to north or south distance. As they sailed north, the constellation rose more nearly overhead. As they sailed south, it sank lower in the sky.

Phoenicians, Polaris was about seven degrees away from celestial north. The Phoenicians took this into account.

The Phoenicians' home ports were in northern Canaan between the cities of Tyre and Sidon north of Mt. Carmel. Today the area is part of Lebanon.

Phoenicia could not have been better located as a crossroads of commerce. The continents of Europe, Africa, and Asia come together there. It borders on the Mediterranean Sea. The Phoenicians became merchants on a grand scale. They established a network of trading stations throughout the Mediterranean shores.

11

They sold cedar from Lebanon and cloth dyed with purple from Tyre. Papyrus came from Egypt; ivory and ebony from Africa. Luxury goods such as silk and spices came from Persia and Asia.

Because of the location near Canaan, the children of Israel often did business with the Phoenicians. For instance, God told Jonah to preach at Nineveh. Jonah instead sought to escape God's command. He took passage on a Phoenician vessel. A ship of Tarshish took him in the opposite direction from Nineveh. A storm overtook the ship. Jonah was thrown overboard where a great fish swallowed him.

Solomon built the Hebrew temple at Jerusalem. He ordered only the best and most costly materials. The temple became the most expensive building ever constructed. Solomon hired Phoenician ships to carry some of the raw materials, such as the cedars of Lebanon. In 1 Kings 5:2, the Bible describes how Solomon asked Hiram, the king of Tyre, to help build the temple.

The people of the ancient world needed bronze for tools and weapons. Bronze is a hard alloy of copper and tin. Copper, although rare, could be found easily enough. But tin was another matter. Few countries had tin mines. The Phoenicians traded in tin. They kept their source a closely guarded secret. They spoke of sailing to the Tin Isles. Perhaps the mysterious Tin Isles were a few islands along the English coast of Cornwall.

Solomon used cedars of Lebanon and other materials from the Phoenicians to build his beautiful temple. The story of the business Solomon conducted with the King of Tyre can be found in I Kings 5:2-12.

If so, the Phoenicians actually sailed through the Strait of Gibraltar and into the Atlantic.

Hanno was a Phoenician navigator with his home port in Carthage, in north Africa. He lived about 530 B.C. He may have been the first European to sail out of the Mediterranean Sea and south along the coast of Africa. Hanno claimed to have discovered islands in the Atlantic and sailed to the southern tip of Africa. Hanno described the noonday sun as being in the northern half of the sky. Impossible, most people thought. They didn't believe his story.

The very part of Hanno's tale that caused doubt in ancient minds caused modern scientists to take it seriously. During summer at noon, the sun is north of the overhead point for people at the equator, exactly as Hanno said. The farther south of the equator you travel, the farther north the sun appears to be. Far south of the equator, the sun is always in the northern part of the sky, even during winter.

In addition, in 1740, a clay pot was uncovered in the Azores, islands far out in the Atlantic. The pot contained coins in common use in Hanno's time.

Most of the Phoenicians stayed within the Mediterranean Sea. The Mediterranean lies between the continents of Africa and

Julius Caesar

Europe. It is huge. It extends from Gibraltar on the west to Syria on the east, a distance of 2,300 miles. Its greatest width, from the head of the Adriatic Sea along Greece to North Africa, is a little over 1,000 miles.

The Strait of Gibraltar connects the Mediterranean Sea to the Atlantic. The Strait narrows to a width of only eight miles. Except for this narrow opening, the Mediterranean is landlocked. It is the largest landlocked sea in the world.

Some of the great cities of the ancient world are found along the Mediterranean: Barcelona in Spain, Naples and Venice in Italy, Marseilles and Nice in France. On its shores along northern Africa are the cities of Algiers, Tunis, Tripoli, and Alexandria.

The Mediterranean Sea is especially kind to sailing ships. It has predictable winds, small tides, and gentle currents. By sailing only in the summer season, ships could leave port and be confident of arriving safely at their destination.

The Mediterranean is not completely safe, especially in winter. The ship taking Paul to trial in Rome delayed too long in seeking a winter harbor. The ship tried to reach a harbor in Crete, but a storm caught it. The ship was destroyed, although no one drowned. Read Acts 27 for an exciting account of what it was like to sail on the Mediterranean during ancient times.

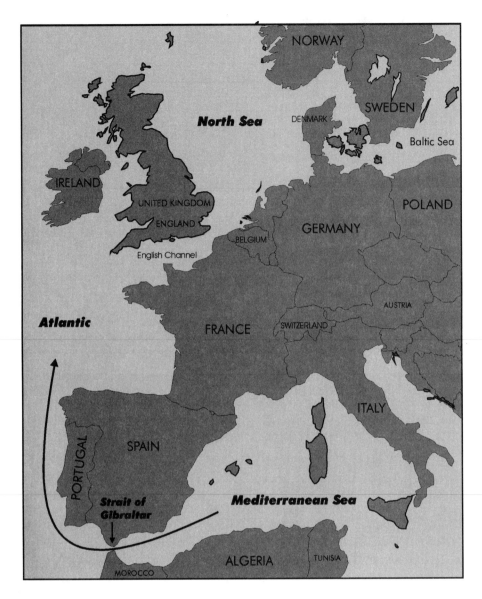

Caesar's sea captains left the Mediterranean to invade England. For the first time they met the stormy conditions of the open sea.

As the fleet approached the English coast, a storm blew up. Winds shredded the sails and snapped the masks. Unexpected high tides dashed his ships against the rocks. Wreckage littered the beaches.

The Romans fought all summer. The dangerous, choppy seas took their toll. With the coming of the winter weather, Caesar crammed his soldiers in the remaining ships. He sailed away, defeated, never to return.

A hundred years passed before the Romans learned enough about the open seas to make a successful invasion of England. This took place during the reign of the emperor Claudius. Claudius is mentioned in the Bible (see Acts 11:28 and Acts 18:2).

Julius Caesar's defeat discouraged sailing outside the Mediterranean. Merchants saw no profit in taking chances with their ships.

Exploration fell into disfavor for another reason. Citizens of Mediterranean countries believed their part of the world to be the center of everything important. The name "Mediterranean" means "middle earth." They thought of themselves as civilized and everyone else as barbarians. What could barbarians possibly trade for the wealth of the Mediterranean? Exploration that began with the Phoenicians came to a halt.

Sailing on the Mediterranean didn't prepare sea captains for the rigors of the open sea. For instance, lack of experience played havoc with Julius Caesar's plans to invade Britain.

Caesar, the Roman emperor, felt confident of the conquest of Britain. He came with 25,000 men, 2,000 horse soldiers, and 800 ships. How could English peasants overcome such might?

Questions

Masters of the Mediterranean

Thought questions:

1. Who were the great explorers and navigators of the ancient world?

_____

_____

2. What are some other names for the Big Dipper?

_____

_____

3. List three of the goods traded in ancient times.

_____

_____

4. Explain why some people believe Hanno sailed into the southern hemisphere.

_____

_____

5. The Bible in Acts 27 describes a ship wreck on what sea?

_____

_____

6. Why did exploration that began with the Phoenicians come to a halt?

_____

_____

MARCO POLO'S BIG ADVENTURE

The Phoenicians explored to open new trade routes. The Greeks explored for military conquest. Later, other civilizations would explore for other reasons — scientific curiosity or to find religious freedom.

Beginning in 100 B.C. Roman civilization, centered in Italy, rose to power. Eventually they would conquer all of the countries that bordered on the Mediterranean. The Mediterranean became the Roman sea, the Mare Nostrum. The words "Mare Nostrum" mean "our sea."

The Romans didn't explore. They were content to take over the trading posts left by the Phoenicians. There was not much new information learned about the earth during Roman times.

The decline of the Roman Empire starting in the 500s brought a drastic change in Europe. Numerous small kingdoms replaced the Roman Empire. The kings engaged in petty feuds with one another. Sometimes a city in one part of the country fought with a city in another part of the same

Antique map of Asia from 1617.

country. City officials grew suspicious of strangers. They threw travelers into prison.

This had a chilling effect upon trade between countries. Commerce and science do go together. When one suffers, so does the other. It is not surprising to learn that during the Dark Ages (from about 550 to about 1450), science in Europe went backwards. People forgot the great gains made by Greek scientists like Eratosthenes and Phoenician explorers like Hanno. The world was again thought of as flat.

About 700 years ago, in the late 1200s, merchants in Venice competed fiercely with each other. They struggled to establish trade with foreign countries. But they dared not venture too far from home.

Then Genghis Khan and his armies swooped out of Mongolia. He captured most of central Asia.

In 1260, Nicolo Polo and his brother Maffeo Polo saw an unusual opportunity. Kublai Khan, the grandson of Genghis Khan, ruled over an immense empire. It covered all

Modern traders travel the Silk Road, the ancient caravan route, as they have done for centuries. Camels still provide a reliable mode of transportation across vast areas of desert. Modern nomads travel the same trails their ancestors did.

of China. His influence extended even farther. Strangers under his protection could safely travel throughout Asia and the Orient.

"The land Kublai Khan rules is rumored to be fabulously wealthy," Nicolo Polo said.

His brother said, "By establishing a trade route with the Khan, we'll be far ahead of the other merchants in Venice."

"Let's travel to China and meet Kublai Khan," Nicolo Polo suggested.

The Polo brothers were among the first Europeans in medieval times to enter China. Kublai Khan received them as royal visitors. He agreed to open China to trade with Europe.

Kublai Khan, ruler of the mongol empire, was also the grandson of Genghis Khan who conquered all of China.

Nicolo and Maffeo Polo returned to Venice. They began preparing for a second trip to China. Marco Polo was Nicolo's fifteen-year-old son. He'd stayed home during the first trip. But not this time. Marco said, "I'm going back to China with you."

At first his father disagreed. Preparations for their return to China took two years. During that time Marco Polo helped. His father came to depend upon him. Marco became so essential to success that Nicolo couldn't leave him behind.

In April of 1271, Marco Polo and his father and uncle set sail from Venice.

The Polos sailed to Palestine, the Holy Land, then headed overland to the east. At first they traveled on horseback. Later, they would ride camels and elephants.

Their journey took them into eastern Turkey. In the distance they saw a mountain with its peak eternally capped in snow. Marco Polo asked a shepherd, "What is the name of the mountain?"

"It is the Mountain of the Ark," the shepherd explained. "High on its peak, Noah's ark came to rest after the flood."

They traveled past Mount Ararat and on to Persia, through Afghanistan, and into western China.

Along the way they came upon the single greatest construction project ever undertaken on the face of the earth: the Great Wall of China. It stretched for 1,800 miles over mountains and across valleys.

The Chinese had built the wall because they feared the savage Mongols to the north. The wall kept China safe from the Mongols for several centuries. But 50 years before Marco Polo began his journey, Genghis Khan, the grandfather of Kublai Khan, united the Mongols. The wall did not stop his army. They swept across most of Asia. Genghis Khan conquered more people and ruled a larger part of the earth's surface than anyone before or since. Kublai Khan took over upon his death.

All along the way Marco Polo made careful notes of the things he'd seen. As they entered a new region, Marco Polo learned the language.

In 1275, after nearly four years, the weary travelers reached Shan-tu, China. Shan-tu, also known as Xanadu (the X is pronounced as a Z), was the summer home of Kublai Khan.

The beautiful summer palace rested in the fresh cool air of the hills. The fabulous Kublai Khan, emperor of all China, welcomed them.

The evident courage and skill of Marco Polo made him a favorite of the Khan. The Kublai Khan had an unusual problem. His empire extended so far he could not possibly hope to visit it all.

The Khan needed a brave man to explore his empire. He hired Marco at once. Marco Polo became a trusted ambassador in Kublai Khan's service. He traveled throughout the vast empire.

During his travels he came across many amazing sights. He saw a fabric that would not burn. Flames could play across the fabric without doing any damage. They called the fabric salamander cloth. A salamander is a real animal. People incorrectly believed the myth that salamanders could live in fire.

Actually, the Chinese made the fabric from the mineral asbestos, a type of rock.

The Chinese used a type of black rock as a fuel. The black stone was coal, of course. They burned it to heat their homes and for cooking. People in Europe still burned wood. A few baked wood to change it into charcoal. Charcoal is cleaner burning and makes a hotter fire. Most Europeans had never seen nor used coal. It did not become a common fuel there for another four hundred years.

Subjects of the Khan also enjoyed an unusual freedom: freedom of religion. In Europe at that time people were expected to worship as their king directed.

"Either follow my example," the king would say, "or face banishment."

In China under the Khan, people could worship in freedom. Christians, Buddhists, and Mohammedans worked together in the Khan's court. The Khan's personal physician was Jewish.

"I protect all religions and allow no intolerance of one religious group against another," the Khan explained.

A sad story comes out of this, too. During their first visit, Nicolo Polo and Maffeo told Kublai Khan about the Christian religion. The subject fascinated the Khan. He didn't believe himself, but he willingly listened to them.

"When you return to Venice," Kublai Khan said, "send a hundred missionaries to instruct my subjects in Christianity."

The Polos presented this invitation to Church leaders, but they acted slowly. Finally, they raised enough money to send two rather timid missionaries to China. The two men had never traveled far. They soon grew discouraged and turned back. The missionaries who Kublai Khan thought were coming, never came.

This failure of nerve lost the great chance to tell the story of Jesus in the Far East.

For 17 years Marco Polo roamed throughout China. He traveled to places as far north as Siberia beyond the Gobi Desert and as far south as Siam. He also traveled on the Yangtze, one of the four great rivers of the world. By his calculations, 200,000 ships passed along it each year.

Finally, the three Polos decided to return home. Kublai Khan asked for one final favor.

Marco Polo's adventures opened up a new world to Europe. Today, he is remembered as one of the great explorers.

The King of Persia asked for a Chinese princess as a bride.

"You, my three friends, will escort the princess to Persia."

"The western border is closed," Nicolo Polo pointed out. "It is too dangerous to travel by land."

"We can go by sea," Marco said.

"Sail?" the Khan asked. "We'll need to build ships and train crews. Marco, I'm putting you in charge of navigating them to Persia."

Marco put together a fleet of 13 ships. They sailed through the Yellow Sea, the China Sea, the Bay of Bengal, over part of the Indian Ocean, through the Arabian Sea, and finally into the Persian Gulf. The distance was 12,000 miles, nearly halfway around the earth.

They delivered the princess safely to Persia. Then, a short overland journey carried them to the Mediterranean Sea. They caught a ship that carried them to Venice.

The Polos made the homeward journey from Peking to Venice in blinding speed. It took only 18 months.

When Marco Polo left home in 1271 he knew that he would be away from home for a long time — maybe 4 years. In actual fact, he was gone for *24 years*.

Marco left as a teenager of 17. He returned as a man of 41.

When the Polos landed in Venice they were wearing their strange-looking and baggy traveling clothes. The family home was still there. So were some of the servants they'd left in charge.

Memory grows dim in 24 years. The servants didn't recognize the Polos. The three men looked like beggars. The servants turned them away.

Marco, his father, and uncle took up residence in a nearby inn. They threw a party and invited all of their old friends and relatives. The Polos unpacked their trunks. They dressed in expensive clothes made of the finest Chinese materials, like silk and satin.

The Polos described their trip in vivid detail. Marco Polo described the Great Wall, paper money, black stones that would burn (coal), cloth that would not burn (asbestos), and hundreds of other marvels. Before the night was over, they'd proven their identity.

Then Nicolo and Maffeo picked up their baggy traveling garments. They cut open the seams. On the table before the startled eyes of their guests a fortune of gems fell out: rubies, emeralds, diamonds, sapphires, and pearls.

The story of Marco Polo's great adventure would probably have been forgotten, but three years later the off and on fighting between the Italian cities of Venice and Genoa began again. During the fighting Marco Polo commanded a Venetian ship. He was captured. He sat out the rest of the war in prison. He shared a cell with an educated man named Rusticiano of Pisa, an able writer. To pass the time, Marco Polo began telling the story of his adventures in China.

His companion in the cell listened in amazement. "Others must hear of this," the man said. "I'll write it down."

Day after day, Marco Polo dictated his story to his companion. This was before the invention of the printing press. As they finished each chapter, copies were written by hand and circulated outside the prison.

People in Genoa read the thrilling story. They could not wait for the next installment. They visited Marco Polo in prison. They listened outside his cell as he told it first hand. Finally, he became so popular he was allowed to live outside the prison. A year later he was allowed to go home.

The Travels of Marco Polo became immensely popular. It was copied by hand and translated into several languages. Even today, over 140 *hand-written* copies of the book are still in existence.

People found the book unbelievable. Indeed, many people didn't believe it. These people said, "Marco's book is nothing more than an entertaining collection of tall tales."

The Great Wall of China in the Pa-ta-ling Area, Shanxi.

Marco described the millions of people who lived in China and the millions of sights he'd seen. He used the word "million" so much people made fun of him and called him "Marco Millions."

Canal in modern Venice.

"Marco invented the whole thing," the people said. "His book is one big lie from beginning to end. A million lies!"

"It is not a lie!" Marco said. "Every word is the truth."

We know now that his book is surprisingly accurate. No one wrote with such sparkle and vigor about China as Marco Polo. No one described what he saw in such detail. Besides, Marco Polo, as the special representative of the Khan, traveled to places closed to others. He alone wrote about the famous city of Shan-tu (Xanadu). Only centuries later did explorers uncover the ruins of that lost city.

No traveler has ever explored a continent so thoroughly. His book became the best source for Europeans to learn about Asia. Mapmakers, merchants, and explorers turned to The Travels of Marco Polo to learn about the Orient.

After Kublai Khan died his great empire fell apart. The route to China became much more dangerous and difficult.

Each king along the route demanded tribute. Only by paying taxes and bribes to tribal chieftains could caravans reach the Far East and return safely. Products like spices and silk that did reach Europe became fearfully expensive.

People today take spices for granted. Spices served two very important purposes during ancient times: First, without refrigeration, meat could not be kept fresh for more than a few days. By the time it reached the dinner table, the meat smelled bad. Spices covered up the bad smell.

Even if the meat was fresh, many people lived on the same food day after day. It was mutton on Monday, mutton on Tuesday, mutton on Wednesday, and so on. By dressing up the dish with a variety of spices, the same food could be given variety. Spices were very important indeed to cooks of the Middle Ages.

People desperately desired the spices of China. A less expensive way of getting them had to be found.

Questions

Marco Polo's Big Adventure

Choose A or B to complete the sentence:

1. The Roman Empire was replaced by
    A. the Industrial Revolution.
    B. numerous small kingdoms.
2. During the Dark Ages, city officials often
    A. greeted strangers as heroes.
    B. threw strangers into prison.
3. In the 1260s China was ruled by
    A. Claudius Caesar.
    B. Kublai Khan.
4. Marco Polo served as Kublai Khan's
    A. ambassador.
    B. doctor.

5. Marco Polo returned to Venice mainly by
    A. a fleet of sailing ships.
    B. the Orient Express Train.
6. Marco Polo had been away from Venice for
    A. 4 years.
    B. 24 years.
7. Marco Polo wrote his book from
    A. the deck of a fighting ship.
    B. a jail cell.

Thought Questions:

8. What are the special properties of asbestos and coal?

_____

_____

9. Why was Marco Polo given the nickname "Marco Millions"?

_____

_____

10. Why were spices so strongly desired by people in Marco Polo's day?

_____

_____

23

CHAPTER 4

THE PORTUGUESE SAIL EAST

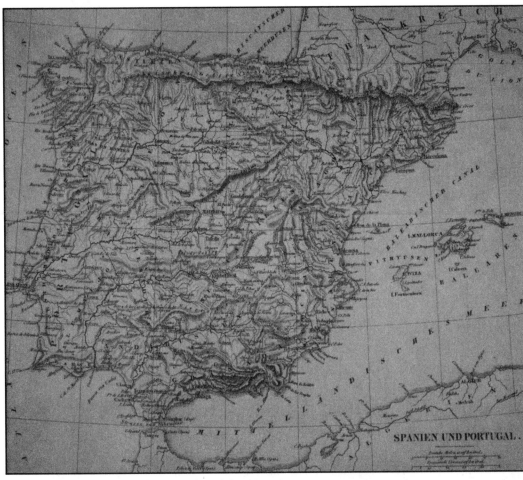

1851 map of Portugal and Spain.

Portugal is the westernmost Mediterranean country. Caravans traveled farther to reach Portugal than to reach any other European country. Because of the great distance and heavy taxes, products that did reach Portugal became fearfully expensive. Sometimes wars closed the land route entirely. Silk and spices could not be bought at any price.

In 1418, Prince Henry of Portugal had an idea. Perhaps the Orient could be reached by sea. He proposed to sail around Africa and to India. No one knew the size of Africa. Going around it might be impossible. The rewards would be worth the effort.

Prince Henry had sailed to Africa only once as a young man

Prince Henry earned the title "Henry the Navigator."

Henry, of course, but his people should still exist.

For all of these reasons — trade with the Orient, exploration of Africa, and the search for Prester John's empire — sailing along the coast of Africa seemed a promising idea.

Until the 1400s, no Europeans dared attempt such a voyage. (Hanno's accomplishments had become lost to the mists of time.) Sailors preferred to stay within the Mediterranean and within sight of land.

John I, Henry's father, was king of Portugal. Prince Henry could have become a powerful ruler or a great military leader. Instead, he devoted himself to the study of sailing. His brother, who was traveling in Italy, sent him a copy of Marco Polo's book. After reading it, Prince Henry became even more determined to reach the Orient.

He pored over maps, geography books, and travel accounts. Court affairs in Lisbon constantly interrupted his studies. Where could he work quietly? He left the pomp and parties of court life. He moved to Sagres, a tiny little town on Cape St. Vincent. It was one of the most desolate spots in Europe, located at the southern tip of Portugal.

At Sagres, he built a small village high on a cliff overlooking the tiny harbor. There he built an observatory and started a school for navigation. The word "navigation" is from a Latin word meaning "to manage a ship," especially directing its course.

during a military campaign. Africa fascinated him. What really lay beyond the Strait of Gibraltar? Where did Africa come to an end? Was it possible to reach India and China by sea?

Exploring Africa captured his imagination for another reason. Christians were believed to live in Africa. Arab lands separated them from Europe. During the 1100s, Europe's Christian rulers sought to make contact with Prester John, a legendary Christian leader. His people were believed to live somewhere in southwest Asia or northeast Africa, just south of the Arab empire. He would be dead by the time of Prince

Prince Henry gathered around him the world's best mapmakers, mathematicians, astronomers, sailors, and ship builders. People who longed for adventure came to

Positions north or south of the equator are measured by parallels of latitude. The equator is 0° latitude. The north pole is 90° north. The south pole is 90° south.

The cross staff was an early navigation tool used to measure latitude.

Sagres and volunteered to serve Prince Henry.

Sagres became a vast storehouse of geographical and scientific knowledge. The sleepy little town soon turned into a bustling port.

Prince Henry explained the goals of his school. "We are to improve the design of ships, make better maps, design navigation instruments, and train sailors in their use."

A ship's position at sea is given by latitude and longitude. The latitude is the distance north or south of the equator. The longitude is the distance east or west from a reference longitude. Today the reference meridian goes through Greenwich, England. It is known as the Prime Meridian.

Sailors of Henry's day used a cross staff to measure latitude. A cross staff is made of two pieces of wood set at right angles to each other. The short piece slides along the longer piece. The navigator puts his eye to the longer stick. He slides the shorter one until the North Star is at its top and the horizon at its bottom.

The angle between the North Star and the horizon is the latitude. If the angle is 18 degrees, then the ship is 18 degrees north of the equator. That's about 1,250 miles.

The sun can be used instead of the North Star, but it's more difficult. The height of the sun above the horizon changes with the time of year as well as with the latitude. It rises higher in the summer and lower in the winter. After sighting the sun, a correction must be added or subtracted to the angle to give the true latitude.

Calculating the correction can be difficult, especially aboard a ship being tossed about on the stormy Atlantic. Besides, sailors weren't mathematicians or astronomers. Many simply didn't have the scientific training needed to make the calculations.

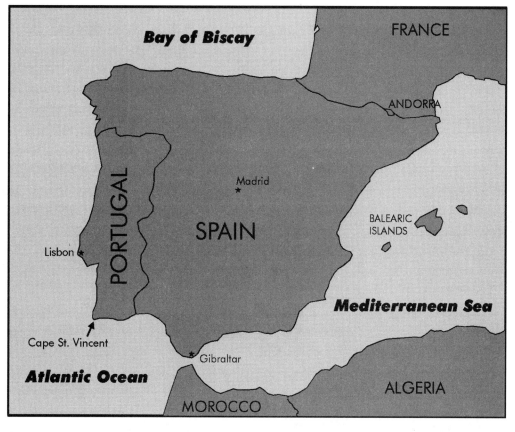

Portugal saw the start of many voyages of discovery. Many brave sailors and ships left Portuguese ports to map "new worlds."

Prince Henry hit upon a solution to the problem. In the comfort and safety of his school, scientists figured the corrections. They wrote the answers into a navigation book. The book contained corrections to the sun's position for every day of the year.

Each ship carried a copy of the book. The navigator "shot the sun" with the cross staff. Then he simply turned to the navigation book and looked up the correction factor. He added or subtracted it from the angle of the sun.

Even with these navigational aids, ship's captains found it difficult to use the cross staff on a tossing ship. Also, "shooting the sun" had to be done precisely at noon, when the sun was at its highest. Most captains made landfall every so often so they could stand on solid land and make their sightings. An error of one degree is 69 miles. Under ideal conditions, a navigator could figure the latitude to within 12 miles — about 1/6 of a degree.

What about longitude? As it turns out, longitude — distance east or west — cannot be figured without an accurate clock. Accurate timepieces did not come into existence until the 1700s. Measuring longitude at sea remained one of the great problems to face explorers for the next 300 years.

Prince Henry spent his personal fortune on the school. Year after year he outfitted ships and sent them out. Each ship probed a little farther down the western coast of Africa.

Worship of God was important to these brave men. Prince Henry built a little chapel at Sagres. The last night before ships departed on their voyage of discovery, special services were held. The crews came to the chapel to pray.

As each captain sailed along he made notes of new landmarks, coastlines, currents, islands, tides, and winds. When he returned home, he gave these notes to the mapmakers who added them to the charts. Each year the charts became more accurate and more dependable.

Henry's navigators achieved their first important success in 1420 when they discovered the island of Porto Santo. The Portuguese sent people to settle the island. The first colonists landed with a pair of rabbits. The rabbits had no natural enemies on the island. They quickly multiplied and overran the island. Colonists planted gardens. The rabbits devoured the young plants as soon as they sprouted. For a time it appeared the Portuguese would have to abandon the island. Finally, however, they brought the rabbits under control.

Ecological disasters like this would happen again. Plants and animals are kept in check by enemies in their natural surroundings. When transported to new locations, they often take over.

Prince Henry's ships continued their voyages of discovery. They found the Azores,

Map of Africa drawn in 1570.

the Canary Islands, and the Cape Verde Islands.

More than 40 years passed. Each ship reported the disturbing news: Africa appeared to have no end. It stretched to the south without end.

Prince Henry refused to give up. He kept after the task with single-minded determination. He earned the title "Henry the Navigator." Except for a short trip to Africa in his youth, Prince Henry never went to sea. Yet, people pointed to him as Portugal's greatest sailor.

Portuguese ships had sailed 2,000 miles along the coast of Africa. Soon they would reach the equator itself. Did the horrible heat predicted by the Greeks await the first ship that dared sail any farther?

The Portuguese rounded the bulge of West Africa and crossed the equator. They returned with good news. "The temperature

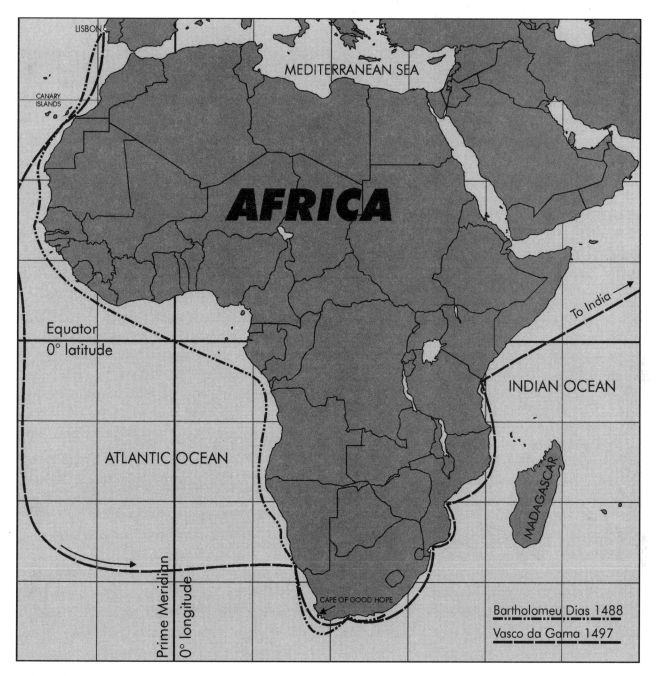

LISBON

MEDITERRANEAN SEA

CANARY ISLANDS

AFRICA

Equator
0° latitude

To India

ATLANTIC OCEAN

INDIAN OCEAN

MADAGASCAR

Prime Meridian
0° longitude

CAPE OF GOOD HOPE

Bartholomeu Dias 1488

Vasco da Gama 1497

Early explorers sailed into uncharted waters and found adventure, hardship, and discovery. The Portuguese were determined to reach India and the spices that would bring their country wealth and power. Prince Henry also wanted to find the lost Christian community founded by Prester John.

is hotter. The sea water is warmer. But the sea does not boil."

The captains also arrived at a disappointing fact. Africa still continued to the south with no break in sight.

Prince Henry died in 1460. Other sailors took up his quest. They became more bold.

Instead of tiny little steps, they sailed down the coast of Africa in giant leaps. In 1488, Bartholomeu Dias, Portugal's most experienced sailor, sailed around the southern tip of Africa. In one trip Dias' ships explored more than a thousand miles of new coast. The tip of Africa was named the Cape of Good Hope.

Vasco da Gama succeed in reaching India.

The Cape of Good Hope is about 35° south latitude, a little over one-third of the way from the equator to the South Pole. The southern tip of Portugal is at 37° north latitude, a little over one-third of the way from the equator to the North Pole. The southern tip of Africa is about as far south of the equator as the southern tip of Portugal is north of the equator. In sailing from Portugal to the Cape of Good Hope, Bartholomeu Dias traveled about one-sixth of the way around the earth.

The king of Portugal ordered an expedition to go all the way to India. He put Bartholomeu Dias in charge of outfitting the expedition. Dias trained the crews, built the ships, ordered the supplies, and planned the route. Putting it all together took ten years.

But for some reason, the king of Portugal did not give the command of the expedition to Bartholomeu Dias. Instead, he put Vasco da Gama in charge of the four-ship fleet.

In 1497 Vasco da Gama sailed from Portugal with a fleet of four ships: *Sao Gabriel, Sao Raphael*, the *Berrio*, and a lumbering cargo ship.

Da Gama refused to waste his time feeling his way along the western coast of Africa. He boldly swooped across the open sea, making landfall just short of the Cape of Good Hope. He rounded the cape and sailed on to India.

The round trip took more than two years. One storm damaged the fleet so badly the supply ship had to be broken apart to repair the others. The men suffered from scurvy, a dreadful disease. Others died from poison arrows during skirmishes with unfriendly natives.

Almost 40 years after Prince Henry's death, Vasco da Gama finally completed the Prince's original goal. The ships Prince Henry sent to explore the coast of Africa began the great age of discovery, which continued for 200 years.

As for Prester John's community of Christians in Africa, their exact location was never found. A small band of Christians did live in Ethiopia. Could these Ethiopian Christians be the remnant of Prester John's kingdom? What happened to them? Did they exist in the first place? It is still a great mystery, even today.

Vasco da Gama's success was tempered with the terrible price the Portuguese sailors paid. Only two of the ships made it back. Two-thirds of the crew died along the way.

By then Columbus had started explorations in the opposite direction — to the west.

Questions

The Portuguese Sail East

Choose A or B to complete the sentence:

1. The distance north or south of the equator is the
    - A. latitude.
    - B. longitude.

2. One of the great problems facing sailors was
    - A. finding their longitude.
    - B. measuring the depth of the sea.

3. At Sagres, the night before sailors left on a long voyage they would
    - A. go to a chapel to pray.
    - B. have a huge party and feast.

4. The Portuguese reached India by sailing to the tip of Africa and heading
    - A. east.
    - B. west.

Thought Questions:

5. Why were spices more expensive in Portugal than in other countries of Europe?

_____

_____

6. Who was Prester John?

_____

_____

7. Why did Prince Henry leave Lisbon?

_____

_____

8. Why did Prince Henry receive the title "Henry the Navigator" although he made but one short sea voyage?

_____

_____

CHAPTER 5

THE SPANISH SAIL WEST

I n 1474, Christopher Columbus read the statement by Eratosthenes: "If the distance were not an obstacle, we might easily pass by sea from Spain to India."

Map of Americas completed in 1733.

If Eratosthenes were correct, southeast Asia (the Indies) would lie 13,000 miles west of Europe. Ships of the 1400s could travel farther than ships during ancient Greek times. But even the best European ships couldn't sail 7,000 miles.

Not everybody agreed with Eratosthenes' value of 25,000 miles for the distance around the earth. Many Greek scholars believed his figure was far too large. It made Greece a small and unimportant country on the face of a vast earth.

Poseidonius (pos-ih-DOH-nee-us), a Greek scholar, re-did the calculations. He arrived at a more satisfying figure of 18,000 miles. The smaller number reduced the surface area of the earth by about half its actual value.

About A.D. 150, Ptolemy, a Greek astronomer, wrote a geography of the known world. (This Ptolemy is not the same as Ptolemy III, the Greek general who put Eratosthenes in charge of the library at Alexandria. Ptolemy the astronomer lived about 350 years after Ptolemy III.) In his geography, Ptolemy quoted the smaller figure for the distance around the earth. Despite its errors, Ptolemy's book remained the best one available for a thousand years. People came to believe the earth was 18,000 miles around.

The land route from Europe to the Indies was 12,000 miles. Sailing around Africa made the trip even longer. Suppose the earth were only 18,000 miles around, as in Ptolemy's book. The Indies would lie only 6,000 miles to the west of Europe across the Atlantic Ocean.

Could the distance be reduced still further? Christopher Columbus thought so. Outlying islands would make the distance even less. Perhaps the Indies lay only 3,000 miles west of Europe.

"Ships like those we have today can make that voyage," Columbus decided. From then on the idea would not die. He'd reach the Indies by sailing west.

Christopher Columbus (Cristoforo Colombo in Italian) was born in Genoa, Italy, in 1451. He went to sea at an early age. His voyages took him down the African coast. He also sailed far to the north to Iceland. There he learned of the legendary Vikings and their stories of land far to the west.

Christopher Columbus, after reading Marco Polo's book, decided he knew a better way to get to Asia.

Columbus hadn't learned to read or write as a child. He learned those skills as an adult when he became interested in sea exploring. He collected the best maps, charts, and travel books.

He read Marco Polo's book time and again and made notes in the margin. In the book, Marco Polo described a great ocean that lay to the east of China. If the world were a sphere, then the ocean to the east of China could be the same as the ocean to the west of Spain.

Columbus sought an audience with King John of Portugal. His country had the biggest ships and best navy.

"I'll reach the Indies by sailing west," Columbus explained. "We all know the

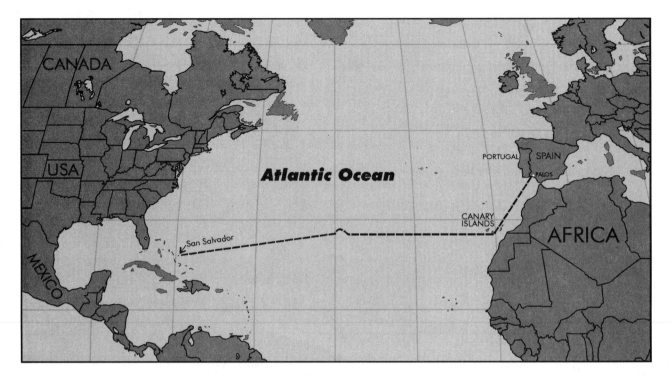

Christopher Columbus set sail from Palos on August 3, 1492, and landed on San Salvador on October 12.

world is round. Therefore, China and India can be reached just as well by sailing west as sailing east."

King John considered the matter. His advisors were against the plan. "Our ships will soon reach the tip of Africa. We are too close to success in that direction to back an untried venture in the other direction."

King John decided against sending his ships in two different directions. "The Portuguese will not be a part of your enterprise," he told Columbus.

Columbus went to Spain, Portugal's chief rival. Spain was a collection of smaller kingdoms. The two strongest rulers were King Ferdinand of Aragon and his wife Queen Isabella of Castile.

He explained his plan to the two monarchs. "We can reach the Indies before the Portuguese," he said. "The shortest route to the Indies is not around Africa but across the Atlantic."

Columbus had piercing gray eyes and flaming red hair. He spoke with his fierce determination. He had total confidence in his ambitious plan.

Despite Columbus' best efforts, it took five years before the two monarchs made up their minds. In 1490 they called him to their court for their decision.

The answer was "no."

Portugal and Spain may have turned him down. But there were other countries — England, France, and Italy. He asked for an audience before their rulers.

Then, Queen Isabella called for him again. "We have changed our minds," she said. "We are pleased to sponsor your voyage."

After 18 years of trying, he had his exploration fleet. But Spain gave him only three small ships: the *Santa Maria*, the *Nina*, and the *Pinta*. The *Santa Maria* was 117 feet long; the other two were only 50 feet long. A ragtag collection of seamen manned the ships. Some, like the three Pinzon brothers, were seasoned sailors. Others were common criminals.

On August 3, 1492, friends and relatives of the crew stood at the dock at Palos. They wept as the ships put out to sea. They didn't expect to see either ships or men again.

Columbus sailed south on a shakedown cruise to the Canary Islands. There he stayed almost a month making changes to the rigging of the ships. He also took aboard enough food and water to last for 40 days.

By sailing south to the Canaries, Columbus was able to find winds that blew regularly to the southwest. In addition to the favorable winds, ocean currents carried the ships along in the direction he wanted to go.

The voyage itself was uneventful except for the frightened and suspicious crew. They threatened mutiny at the slightest sign of trouble. For 30 days they were out of sight of land. The crew became more jittery.

On the morning of October 11, sailors noticed twigs floating on the crests of waves. Huge flocks of birds could be seen flying to the southwest.

Columbus took heart. Land could not be far off. That night he stood on deck of his command ship, the *Santa Maria*. His eyes strained into the darkness. His ears listened for the sound of waves breaking upon shore. Shortly after midnight he sighted light, a camp fire.

"Praise be to God!" Columbus said. "Take in the sails. We'll wait for daylight to make landfall."

The next morning, Columbus stepped ashore on a small island. He fell to his knees, kissed the earth, and gave thanks to God.

He named the island San Salvador, which means "the Saviour."

Christopher Columbus was deeply religious. One of the reasons for his voyage was to carry Christianity to other people. He believed that mission was as important as finding gold and spices of the Indies.

Land was a welcome sight

From San Salvador, he sailed on to discover Cuba and Hispaniola (Haiti and the Dominican Republic). Columbus believed the islands to be outlying islands of the Indies. He thought he'd reached his goal. He gave the islands the name "West Indies." He called the natives who lived there "Indians."

But something was wrong — badly wrong. Instead of fabulous cities of ancient China, India, or Japan, he found only endless miles of sand and poor natives. Rather puzzled, he set sail back to Spain.

The homeward voyage proved more difficult than the original trip. His ships fought strong head winds and contrary currents. Finally, he sailed north and caught a west wind bearing toward Europe.

Columbus reported to King Ferdinand and Queen Isabella. The Spanish monarchs decided to start a colony in the new lands.

The next year Columbus returned to the West Indies. He commanded 17 ships carrying 1,500 people. He served as governor of the Spanish colony. He helped start Santo Domingo, the first permanent European settlement in the New World.

Columbus proved a much better sailor and navigator than a government official. His sailing kept him away from his political duties. Those he put in charge while he was away ruled even more poorly. Conditions became so bad that the colonists complained to Spain. A royal official investigated. He ordered Columbus bound in chains and sent back to Spain.

Amerigo Vespucius gave his name to the new land.

Christopher Columbus, Spain's most famous and successful explorer, arrived in court in chains. That sad event was soon forgotten, and Columbus once again set out on a voyage of discovery.

He made four voyages to the West Indies. No other sailor had the knowledge or the courage to sail thousands of miles into the unknown the way Columbus did. His navigating skill became legendary.

Once he crossed the Atlantic and missed his intended landfall by only 35 miles.

When he died in 1506 Columbus was planning still another voyage to find the Asian mainland. As it turned out, Columbus had the wrong figure for the size of the earth. The earth was 25,000 miles around, not 18,000. The extra 7,000 miles left enough room for the American continents. Columbus had discovered a "new world" not on any maps. He himself died without ever learning the truth about his discovery.

It is good for Columbus that he did find land between Spain and Asia. His ships would never have been able to cross an ocean 7,000 miles across.

In 1507, Amerigo Vespucius (ves-PYOO-shus), an Italian navigator of Florence, explored the South American coasts. Amerigo convinced the mapmakers that the land was not China, India, or Japan, but a whole new world. Martin Waldseemuller, a mapmaker, gave the name "America" to the new land.

When the Spanish rulers learned the truth they were intensely disappointed. They considered Columbus a failure because he'd not found a way to the riches of Asia. Of course, within a few years the Americas became more important and valuable than the route to India.

Questions

The Spanish Sail West

Choose A or B to complete the sentence:

1. In preparing for his sea voyages, Columbus
    - A. ignored all the discoveries made before his time.
    - B. studied the best maps, charts, and books, including those of Ptolemy and Marco Polo.

2. When Columbus stepped ashore in the new world he
    - A. built a monument to himself and Queen Isabella.
    - B. fell to his knees and gave thanks to God.

3. The first island he called San Salvador which means
    - A. "salt is here."
    - B. "the Saviour."

4. Columbus was better as a
    - A. governor.
    - B. sailor.

5. Columbus once appeared in court
    - A. as king of the new world.
    - B. in chains.

6. The new world received the name America from
    - A. Columbus' mother's maiden name.
    - B. Amerigo Vespucius, an Italian navigator.

Thought Questions:

7. Why did Columbus think the route west to India would be shorter than the one east around Africa?

_____

_____

8. Why did friends and relatives of Columbus' crew weep as they put out to sea?

_____

_____

CHAPTER 6

SAILING AROUND THE WORLD

Columbus is said to have discovered the New World, even though he was not the first European to cross the Atlantic. The Vikings reached the New World in the year 1000.

It began with Eric the Red who was born in Norway in the 900s. Eric the Red came from Viking chieftains. He grew up in Iceland. He was banished from Iceland for taking the life of another human being. He sailed westward from Iceland and discovered a large island. He called it Greenland. He chose that name to make it sound attractive to future settlers.

Some people consider Greenland an island of North America. In that case Eric the Red was the first European to land in the New World.

The world as seen in 1587.

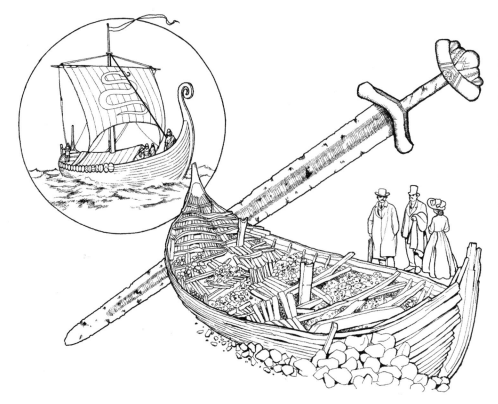

In 1880 a very well-preserved Viking ship was found near Oslo, Norway. It is called the Gokstad ship. It had been a strong, slender warship.

1500s the climate changed for the worse. Winters became severe, The ground froze. Crops couldn't be planted. Eventually, the colony faded away. Those who didn't die sailed back to Iceland.

Despite all of these voyages by the Vikings, Columbus is still said to have discovered America. A discovery in the scientific sense means to make information available to a wider audience. When a person makes a discovery, but keeps it secret, then it's not a discovery at all.

After exploring along the coasts of Greenland, Eric sailed back to Iceland. He organized an expedition to settle the new land. In 985 he returned to Greenland with 25 ships carrying people to start a permanent colony.

Eric's wife was a Christian. She helped build a Christian church in Greenland in 1000.

Leif Eriksson, Eric's son, grew up on Greenland. In 999 he visited Norway. Like his mother he was a Christian, and King Olaf I sent him on a mission to Greenland. A storm blew Leif Eriksson off course. His ship missed Greenland and instead landed along the North American coast.

He called the new land Vinland. The exact location of Vinland is not known. It may have been Newfoundland or Labrador. Leif Eriksson spent the winter of 1000 in Vinland. Then he sailed to Greenland.

The colony and Christian community did survive on Greenland for 500 years. In the

Columbus, not Leif Eriksson, gets credit for discovering America in the scientific sense. Columbus understood the importance of his discovery and told others of it. It was the voyage of Columbus that opened the New World to further exploration.

Eleven years after the death of Columbus, a Portuguese navigator named Ferdinand Magellan (ma-JEL-an) sought to prove Columbus right after all. Ferdinand Magellan spent years in loyal service to Portugal. He kept waiting for his big chance. Other captains always seemed to get the better assignments.

In 1517, Magellan left Portugal and offered to sail under the Spanish flag. "I can reach the Indies without going around Africa," he told them. "I'll sail around the Americas and keep on going."

Spain and Portugal had been rivals for many years. To avoid trouble, the ships of the two countries were kept apart by a political agreement. Portugal stayed east of a certain line down the middle of the Atlantic, and Spain stayed west. Essentially, the two "super powers" split the earth in half.

The agreement cut Spain out of the race to India by way of Africa. Portugal could trade with the East Indies, but Spain couldn't. Spain had no choice but to continue its exploration of the New World and hope to discover riches there.

Magellan's plan was simple. Sail west to South America and then sail south until he found a way around it. In 1519, Magellan organized a fleet of five ships. He probed along the coast of South America for a way through. At 35 degrees south latitude, the latitude at which da Gama found his way around Africa, South America showed nothing but solid land. Magellan continued south.

Finally he came to a break in the land and entered it. He traveled through a passage that is today called the Strait of Magellan. Swells, wind-whipped waves, and wild storms threatened the fleet. As it turned out, the weather in the strait is seldom any better. The passage is one of the most difficult tests of navigating skill on earth. Magellan and his ships spent 38 days working through the 360-mile strait. Later, other ships would spend 60 days or more feeling their way through the confusing channels.

The Strait of Magellan opened onto a new ocean. In comparison to the terrible storms Magellan had just survived, the ocean seemed very peaceful indeed. He gave it the name Pacific, meaning "peaceful."

Magellan sailed into a vast and empty sea. For 98 days he sailed without sighting land — twice as long as it took to cross the Atlantic. It became clear that this body of water was the earth's largest ocean.

Magellan passed the point of no return. He simply didn't have enough supplies to retrace his route. Magellan had no choice but to sail on. The ships ran out of food and water. The men were reduced to eating the oxhide fittings on the sails.

Then, when all seemed lost, they reached Guam, an isolated and small island. They took on provisions.

Magellan and his crew sail from Spain on September 20, 1519. Only one of the ships, the Victoria, would return.

The next landfall was the Philippines. There Magellan unwisely involved himself in a squabble between two native tribes. He met his death in the fighting.

Magellan began his voyage with five ships. One ship ran aground and was wrecked while scouting the eastern coast of South America. The crew of another ship gave up the mission while in the Strait of Magellan. They overcame their captain and fled back to Spain with most of the food and supplies. By now there were too few men to man three ships. One ship was taken apart and used to repair the others.

The two remaining ships, the *Victoria* and the *Trinidad*, continued westward across the Indian Ocean. They reached Africa, sailed around it, and sailed on. Along the coast of Africa, the Portuguese captured the *Trinidad*.

On September 8, 1522, a single ship, the *Victoria*, dropped anchor at home in Spain. Sebastin del Cano (KAH-noh) commanded the ship. He and his crew became the first to circumnavigate (sail around) the earth. They'd proved the earth was a sphere — and a large one.

It was a costly triumph. Five ships and 280 men set out on the three-year voyage. Only one ship and 18 sick and half-starved seamen made it home.

Sebastin del Cano summed it up: "The Pacific Ocean is so vast that the mind of man could scarce grasp its magnitude."

Spanish and Portuguese ships were equipped with crude navigating aids, such as compasses, quadrants, and hourglasses. These were simply inadequate for the challenge before them.

Ferdinand Magellan

Longitude, for instance, is very difficult to measure without an accurate clock. (Why this is so will be described in a later chapter.) The difficulties of measuring longitude were so great that tiny islands in the vast Pacific were found, lost, and found again.

Successful exploration demanded more than brave captains and crews. Sailors needed to understand the forces that put trade winds into motion and caused ocean currents. They needed to understand how the earth's magnetic field caused a compass to point north. They needed accurate clocks and reliable tide tables.

These tools of modern navigation would take more than 200 years to develop.

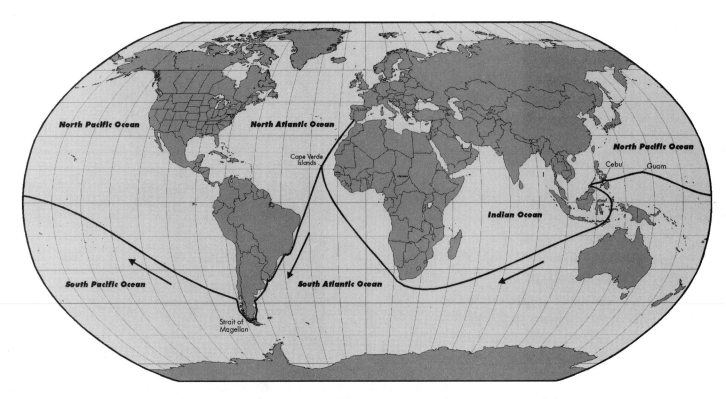

The first voyage around the world began on September 20, 1519, with five ships and ended on September 6, 1522, with only one ship remaining.

Magellan and his men sailed with a fleet of five ships, believing they would soon be home with their families. They sailed across the Atlantic, landing on the coast of Brazil. They spent several months searching for a strait through the mainland. (A strait is a fairly narrow passageway connecting two large bodies of water.) Bitterly cold weather forced them to stop for the winter on the coast of what is now Brazil.

In the spring Magellan entered the strait at the tip of South America in the Atlantic Ocean. While trying to navigate through it, the crew of one ship mutinied. The rebel crew sailed back toward Spain with over one-third of the food and supplies. Magellan waited several days for their return. Finally, he returned to the task of seeking a way through the watery channel. After 38 days he emerged into the Pacific Ocean. He probably thought the worst was behind him. He had no way of knowing the largest ocean in the world lay before him.

Questions

Sailing Around the World.

Choose A or B to complete the sentence:

1. Eric the Red was
   - A. an Italian.
   - B. a Viking.
2. Eric the Red discovered the island of
   - A. Greenland.
   - B. Zanzibar.
3. The land Leif Eriksson called Vinland was probably along
   - A. the North American coast.
   - B. islands north of Scotland.
4. The colony on Greenland died out after 500 years because of
   - A. a change in climate.
   - B. war.

5. The Straits of Magellan are at the southern tip of
   - A. Africa.
   - B. South America.
6. The Straits of Magellan are so
   - A. storm-tossed they test a sea captain's skill.
   - B. peaceful they were given the name Pacific.
7. Magellan did not complete his around the world trip because
   - A. he gave up and turned back.
   - B. he died during the fighting between two native tribes in the Philippines.

Thought Questions:

8. Why are the Vikings not given credit for the scientific discovery of the new world?

_____

_____

9. What more does successful exploration require than brave captains and crews?

_____

_____

CHAPTER 7

THE TEN THOUSAND NAMES OF WIND

The importance of something can be judged by the number of names for it. Important things have many names. In the English language we have hundreds of names for wind. (Can you think of some?) All of the languages of the world together have more than ten thousand names for wind.

Wind may be so gentle it feels like a feather across one's cheek. In New England this breeze is called a Cat's Paw because it barely ripples

The people of the Netherlands have understood the power of the wind and have used it for centuries.

Today's version of the windmill is called a wind turbine generator. As their blades turn, wind is converted into electricity. It is estimated that by the middle of the next century 10 percent of all the world's electricity will come from these wind turbine generators. Denmark is now getting 2 percent of its power from them. They are also being used on several islands and remote locations that would otherwise have a hard time getting electricity. When several are erected together the area is referred to as a wind farm. The world's largest wind farms are in California.

the surface of ponds — like a cat playing with its reflection in the water. In Portugal the same easy breeze is called *vento coado.* In Japan it is called *soya kaze.* Hawaii has a light wind called *kohilo.*

Some winds are extremely dry. In the United States the famous *Santa Ana* falls from the high slopes of the Rocky Mountains. As it falls it dries out and grows hotter. In Canada, the same dry, hot wind from the Rockies is called a *chinook.* It is welcome because the chinook thaws out the cold of winter. For a few days the weather is like spring.

But early settlers crossing the deserts of North America in wagon trains dreaded the Santa Ana. When it struck it burned the eyes with sand, scorched throats, and dried lips. Oxen and horses had to be protected with blankets. Wooden wagon wheels had to be tarred to keep them from drying out and splitting.

The drying effects of a hot wind are illustrated in the Bible in Genesis 8:1. God made a wind to pass over the earth and dry it after the flood.

In the deserts of Africa, the *simoom,* or "burning wind," is hot and dry. Herodotus, the Greek historian, tells of the ancient people of Tripoli who suffered from a long simoom. Their wells dried up. The people declared war on the simoom. They gathered their weapons and marched into the Sahara. With clashing cymbals and beating drum they disappeared into the swirling sand, never to be seen again.

Some winds bring rain. The best known is the *monsoon* of India. During the monsoon season, fields are flooded and roads become mired with mud. The monsoon is necessary because rice, an important food crop in India, must have plenty of water to grow.

Germany has a rainy wind called *steppenwind*. Hawaii has a cold, wet wind called *waimea*. In the United States, sailors know to head for a safe harbor when they sight a fast-moving rainy wind called a *squall*.

Some windstorms come without warning. In the level midwestern plains of the United States wind is able to travel for a thousand miles without a mountain to slow it down. Like a giant roller the wind moves faster and faster. It rolls across the prairie at 100 miles an hour. Suddenly it strikes a farm and rips up roofs, topples grain elevators, and carries away tons of topsoil.

Other countries have names for these sudden windstorms. Australia calls it a *willy-willy*. Scotland calls it the *landlash*.

What is wind? Wind is simply air in motion. Two forces cause air to move: convection currents and the rotation of the earth.

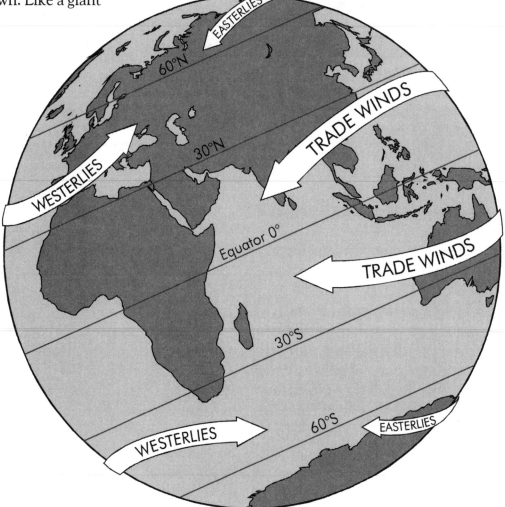

The winds of the earth are affected by many things. The 23.5 degree tilt of the earth's axis, the 360 degree rotation every 24 hours, the latitude, even the shape of the mountains all cause the winds to change or act differently. These are just a few of the forces that affect the direction and force of global and local winds. No wonder weather forecasting is so complicated.

God not only gave birds the ability to fly, but to soar on the wind. This red tail hawk is a joy to watch.

Convection is the movement of heat by currents within a substance. Most substances grow lighter as they are heated. The warmer material rises to be replaced by cooler material.

Convection takes place better in some substances than in others. The tiny particles of matter, atoms, and molecules, that form solids are locked into place. The particles cannot flow. For that reason, convection cannot take place in solids. But the atoms and molecules of a liquid or gas can move around. Convection occurs best in liquids like water and in gases like the atmosphere.

As an example of convection, consider a burning candle. The flame heats the air and it expands. The warmer air rises to be replaced from below by cooler air. The cooler air also brings in a fresh supply of oxygen. A candle flame flickers even in a room with still air. Rising convection currents blow the flame back and forth, causing the flickering.

Hot air rises, cool air falls. A thermal is a hot updraft of air. On a day when the air is still, you can fly a kite if you catch it in a rising current. Sail planes and gliders remain aloft by choosing these rising columns of air. Birds like the condor, eagle, and albatross fly hundreds of miles by moving from one thermal to another.

Hot air that spirals up as it rises creates a whirlwind. In Japan the whirlwind is called *tsumuji*, and in Africa it is called *habob*. Another name for it in the United States is the *dust devil*.

A whirlwind seldom causes damage. Not so with a tornado. A tornado is the most violent of all winds. Tornadoes, or twisters, usually spin out of thunderstorms when the air is unstable. A tornado lives for only a few minutes. Although it is small, less than 200 yards across, it spins with incredible speed. The exact speed has been impossible to measure. Whenever weather instruments are in the path of a tornado they have been ripped away. But most scientists believe air speed at the center of a tornado is more than 600 miles an hour.

Other names for tornado are *waterspout* (if it is over the ocean) and *cyclone*.

Convection has far-reaching importance to human beings. On a small scale, convection currents keep fires burning and bring fresh air into buildings. On a large scale, they produce winds and ocean currents.

Sea breezes are produced by convection. During the day, a sea breeze blows into the shore from off the ocean. At night, the wind reverses direction. It flows from land to sea. Why the change?

When water and land are heated by sunlight, the land warms more quickly than the water. During daytime, air over the land

47

The other force that causes wind is the rotation of the earth upon its axis. A point on the rim of a wheel travels a greater distance than a point nearer the center of the wheel. In the same way, air near the equator moves faster than air near the poles.

This rotation causes westerly winds (wind from out of the west) near the equator. Farther north, prevailing easterly winds are formed. The prevailing easterlies and westerlies are

The hurricane above is viewed from space. Seeing the curve of the earth puts its size into perspective. To the right, another massive storm is seen from the open cargo bay of the space shuttle.

is heated and rises. Cooler air from over the sea flows in to take its place. The breeze blows from sea to land.

At night, the situation is reversed. The land cools more quickly than the sea. Warmer air over the sea rises. Cooler air from over the land flows in to take its place. The breeze blows from land to the sea.

Usually, these sea breezes are gentle. England has a sea breeze so nice and refreshing it is called "the Doctor."

People have harnessed the power of the wind for thousands of years for work and play.

very predictable and dependable. Sailors call these winds trade winds because sailing ships could travel both ways across the ocean by catching the right trade wind.

The famous navigators of the Age of Exploration soon learned about the prevailing winds on the ocean's surface. But Prince Henry, Columbus, and Magellan were earthbound. What about winds higher in the sky?

Until the late 1700s, scientists could not explore into the atmosphere. Their only clue to winds aloft came from watching how clouds drifted about. Then, with the invention of the balloon by the Montgolfier brothers and the airplane by the Wright brothers, exploring the atmosphere became possible.

The first balloonists explored three miles into the earth's atmosphere. They encountered winds far more fierce than those on the surface. The gentle clouds drifting across the

sky turned out to be an illusion. Instead, winds whip the clouds along. Winds above the surface of the earth are usually twice as fast as winds along the surface.

Hidden in the sky were two rivers of wind, the jet streams. Until their discovery, no one imagined their existence, or that they could travel so fast.

In 1940, pilots flying high across the Pacific sometimes found their planes motionless. The planes were inside a jet stream. A jet stream is a fast-moving current of air that travels from west to east at a height of five to ten miles, encircling the earth. Usually, the Northern Hemisphere has two jet streams — one that flows across the southern part of the United States and another that is farther north. The Southern Hemisphere has jet streams in similar positions.

The jet streams are caused by the rotation of the earth. Their speed varies some, but can be as high as 500 miles per hour. Weathermen believe the jet streams are responsible for much of the general weather of the earth. Jet streams carry heat and energy all around the earth.

The jet streams are like rivers of air. Like rivers, they meander about with great bends and horseshoe loops in their paths. Under certain conditions, kinks in the jet stream may break away. A hurricane forms. The wind inside a hurricane is as powerful as the jet stream itself. A hurricane is also known as a typhoon.

A hurricane is the most powerful storm known. Its winds are not as violent as those of a tornado, but the hurricane is thousands of times larger. It may be 500 miles across.

Hurricanes and tornadoes can be deadly. But just as deadly as a windstorm is no wind at all.

Convection currents replace stale air over cities with fresh air. The ground is heated by sunlight. Air near the ground becomes warm and rises, causing a natural air flow, and refreshes the air over a city.

> *The importance of something can be judged by the number of names for it. Important things have many names. . . . All of the languages of the world together have more than ten thousand names for wind.*

Warm air is usually found near the ground and cooler air at higher altitude. But during a temperature inversion a warm upper layer of air covers a valley. The warm air acts as a lid, keeping polluted air within the valley. When the air above a city doesn't move, there is no wind, and the city becomes blanketed by an unpleasant — and dangerous — cover of smog. Each day that the air is still, fumes from automobiles and smoke from factories spew into the air.

One of the most dangerous smogs of all time blanketed London in 1952. The air became so thick darkness fell at noon. Automobiles drove with their lights on. Breathing became difficult. Older people had to avoid exercise. Schools canceled outside recess. People going outside tried to breath by wearing handkerchiefs over their faces.

Airplane pilots who flew over the city reported that it looked like a great silent sea of gray smoke. From the airplane only the tops of higher buildings could be seen. More than 4,000 people died. The lack of wind can be deadly.

What solved this problem? A wind! A gentle breeze, hardly enough to make leaves wiggle, began blowing. Its invisible force gently brushed away the stale air and replaced it with fresh. Winds swept the air clean.

Sailors have a name for the lack of wind — the doldrums.

Questions

The Ten Thousand Names of Wind

Match each type of wind with an example:

1. gentle
2. dry
3. rain
4. windstorm
5. whirlwind
6. tornado
7. hurricane

a. cat's paw
b. dust devil
c. monsoon
d. Santa Ana
e. twister
f. typhoon
g. willy-willy

Choose A or B to complete the sentence:

8. The two forces that cause air to move are convection currents and

    A. radiant energy.

    B. rotation of the earth.

9. Sea breezes are caused by

    A. convection.

    B. tides.

CHAPTER 8

THE MYSTERY OF TIDES

It is customary to begin study of a scientific topic by describing what the Greeks thought about the subject. In the case of tides, however, the Greeks made no discoveries. They didn't speak about tides because they didn't know about them.

Waves from the incoming tide crash against a rock on California's central coast.

The Greeks lived on the shores of the Mediterranean Sea. The Mediterranean Sea is practically landlocked. The surge of a high tide from the ocean is filtered out as it tries to squeeze through the Strait of Gibraltar. Tides of the Mediterranean Sea are too slight to be noticed under ordinary circumstances.

The Romans fared no better than the Greeks. Julius Caesar had a string of military victories until he sailed out of the Mediterranean Sea to invade England. He anchored his ships near land during low tide. The tide turned and smashed the ships against the rocky shores. The invasion failed.

A lack of knowledge about tides can lead to disaster. After explorers ventured out of the Mediterranean Sea, they tried to improve their knowledge of tides. The subject proved difficult to master.

Tides are difficult to predict. No two are alike. They come at different times in different ports.

Navigators did prepare tide tables for busy ports. But winds and weather conditions often threw the tide tables in error, or made them seem in error. During a storm when the air pressure is low, the ocean bulges up. When the air pressure is high, the extra weight of the air presses down on the water. This lowers the sea level. Strong winds interfere with tide predictions, too.

Understanding tides is much more difficult than one might think at first. Real progress could only be made when the reason for tides was understood. But even at the time of Columbus, scientists did not know what caused tides.

Some facts did strongly point to the moon's influence. For example, observe a tide at the same point for a few days. During a 24-hour period there is a high-low-high-low tide cycle. However, the cycle is not

Sir Isaac Newton, a devoted Christian, is considered to be the greatest genius of all time.

exactly 24 hours. Instead, it is 24 hours 50 minutes. The moon rises 50 minutes later each day.

Yet, the high tide is not necessarily directly under the moon. It may lag behind by as much as six hours. There is a second high tide opposite the earth from the first. How could there be two high tides and only one moon?

All this makes the tides quite irregular and hard to tie in with the regular motion of the moon.

Galileo, the great Italian scientist, found it hard to imagine a real connection between the moon and tides. He considered all of the facts and dismissed the moon as the cause of tides.

53

It was only in 1684 that Isaac Newton gave the correct explanation for tides. He worked out the theory of gravitation and showed that the pull of the moon and the sun on the earth could account for the tides.

Isaac Newton was born on a cold Christmas Day in 1642 outside the English town of Woolsthorpe. He was much too underweight, and he had an oversized head and undersized body. It didn't seem the boy would have much of a chance of accomplishing anything in the world. His father had died before his birth, and his mother lived in poverty.

The baby barely clung to life. Neighbors came to comfort the mother. They prayed that the baby would survive to see the new year. Isaac Newton didn't die. He managed to live through that first Christmas. As the weeks passed he grew in strength.

He seemed hardly different from other children his age. He did enjoy working with his hands. He drew pictures and enjoyed copying favorite passages from the Bible. He built all sorts of interesting gadgets. He made kites, clocks that kept time, and a toy windmill that actually ground wheat into flour.

Isaac Newton studied theology and mathematics at Cambridge University. He graduated in 1665 without any particular honors.

Shortly after graduation, and before he had time to find a position at the university as a teacher, an epidemic struck. The Black Death — bubonic plague — raged throughout London and Cambridge. Officials of the university closed its doors until the epidemic passed.

Isaac Newton returned to his mother's farm. For more than 18 months he enjoyed leisure time and quiet surroundings. He began to think deeply about many of the

Edmund Halley applied Newton's laws of motion to all available information on comets. He then correctly predicted the return of a comet in 1758.

problems his teachers had mentioned during the science classes.

He wondered why the moon circled the earth and did not fly out into space.

During good weather he set a study table and chair in an apple orchard. One day an apple fell from a tree and banged on his work table in the orchard. He picked up the apple, and as he held it, he noticed the half-full moon which had risen.

He had an inspiration. The moon didn't fly out into space because it, like the apple, was held in place by a pull of the earth's gravity.

He tested his idea by a rough calculation of the moon's motion. The answer was off a little, so Isaac Newton put the calculations aside. He went on to other matters. In the space of a few months, Isaac Newton made breakthroughs in mathematics, astronomy, light and color, and physics.

What accounted for his success? Newton didn't work by sudden inspiration. Instead, he constantly thought about the problem, until, "little by little, it dawns into a full and clear light."

When Cambridge opened again, Newton's mathematics teacher, Isaac Barrow, saw Newton's genius. He stepped down and gave his job to Newton.

Almost 20 years passed. In 1684 a young astronomer named Edmund Halley called upon Isaac Newton. (This is the same Halley who would later have Halley's Comet named in his honor.)

Isaac Newton and Edmund Halley became good friends. After studying Newton's work, Halley realized that Isaac Newton knew far more about scientific subjects than any living person.

"You must publish a book that details all of your important discoveries," Edmund Halley insisted.

Isaac Newton agreed. Although Newton based his book upon 20 years of work, the actual writing took 18 months. These 16-hour days were filled with the most exhausting mathematical calculations and intricate logical constructions.

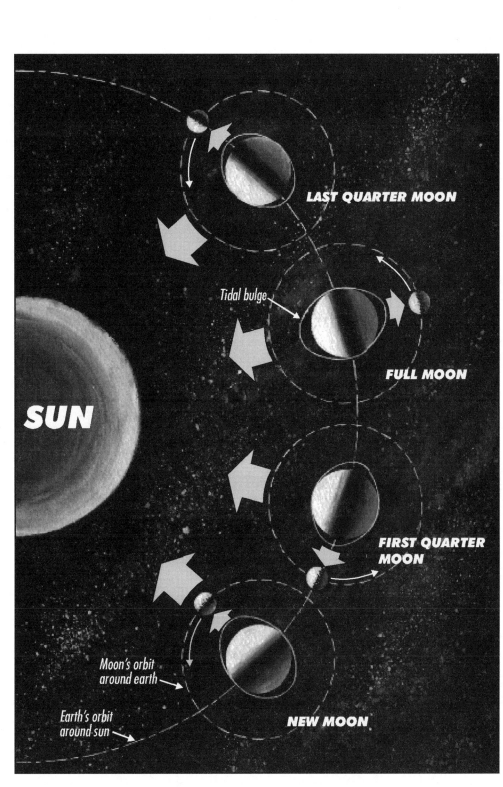

LAST QUARTER MOON

Tidal bulge

FULL MOON

SUN

FIRST QUARTER MOON

Moon's orbit around earth

Earth's orbit around sun

NEW MOON

Lunar and solar tides – the moon, being much nearer to the earth is the main cause of tides. When the moon is over a certain part of the earth it puts a powerful pull on the water and causes a high tide. There is also a high tide on the opposite side of the earth. The sun also pulls at the water, but because the sun is farther from the earth, its tide-raising force is only about 46 percent that of the moon.

Wave action has carved a natural bridge at Four Mile Beach, California.

Isaac Newton's book, the *Principia*, is the most important science book ever published. In it he stated the law of universal gravitation. He showed how gravity keeps the planets in their orbit about the sun, and the moon in orbit about the earth.

Tides, Newton showed, are caused by the force of gravity upon the ocean. The moon's gravity attracts two heaps of water on opposite sides of the earth. As the earth rotates, these bulges of water stay in place. But to a person on the surface of the earth, the bulges of water seem to move as the earth rotates.

The high tides are not directly under the moon due to friction along the ocean's floor. The amount of friction depends upon the depth of the sea and the shape of the shoreline. The time that tides lag behind the moon varies from one place to another.

Why two heaps of water? Why not only one on the side facing the moon? The reason is complicated and depends upon more than one factor. The moon's orbit is mostly over the equator. Water near the poles is pulled down closer to the equator to be nearer the moon. Water on the far side of the earth is affected by this pull, too.

The portion of ocean nearest the moon is pulled extra hard because it is nearer, so it rises in a high tide. The ocean farthest from the moon is pulled less because it is farther away. The water on the far side of the earth is not acted upon as strongly by the moon's gravity as the water on the near side. The water on the far side of the earth is "left behind."

Isaac Newton showed that tides are not caused entirely by the moon. The sun enters the picture, too. The sun is heavier than the moon, so its gravity is bigger. But the sun is much farther away as well. For that reason, the sun's gravity does not affect tides as much as does the moon. The tidal forces due to the sun are about half those due to the moon.

Highest high tide and lowest low tide occur one after another when sun, moon, and earth are in approximately a straight line. This happens twice each month: once during full moon and during new moon. These exceptionally large tidal ranges are called *spring* tides. Despite the name, spring tides occur all year long, not just during the spring. The smallest tides occur when the sun and moon cancel each other. This occurs during first quarter moon and third quarter moon. These weak tides are called *neap* tides.

In 1696, at the age of 54, Newton moved to London. He became Master of the Mint. His job was to reform the coinage of England. The post required skill, knowledge of metals, absolute honesty, and the trust of the people. As England's recoinage plans took effect, 60,000 pounds of silver passed through his control each *week*.

British scientists elected him permanent president of the Royal Society. The Royal Society was the first group of scientists to meet on a regular basis. Fellow professors chose him to represent them in Parliament.

But his greatest honor came in 1705 when Queen Anne knighted him. As Sir Isaac Newton he became the first person to receive knighthood for scientific achievement.

During the London years, he brought out the revised edition of *Principia*. He was aghast at those scientists who used his law of universal gravitation to present the universe as only some sort of great clock.

So that his *Principia* would not be misused, Newton added a section to the second edition that reads in part: "This most beautiful system of the sun, planets, and comets could only proceed from the counsel and dominion of an intelligent and powerful Being."

Isaac Newton was an extraordinary person, the greatest scientist who ever lived. But the extraordinary fact is this: science was not Newton's chief interest. Instead, he had a passion for Bible study. He spent more time studying the Bible during his life than he did investigating nature. He read the Bible, took thousands of pages of notes, wrote religious tracts, and two books on religious subjects: *The Prophecies of Daniel* and *Chronology of Ancient Kingdoms*.

Tidal Pools are a rich source of food for local wildlife.

When Newton died in 1727, his countrymen buried him among kings and generals at Westminster Abbey. The memorial reads: "Mortals! Rejoice at so great an ornament to the human race."

Isaac Newton is considered the greatest genius of all time; yet, Newton realized that science wasn't enough. He once said, "The great ocean of truth lay all undiscovered before me."

William Wordsworth, the poet, described Isaac Newton as "a mind forever voyaging though strange seas of thought, alone."

During his life, Isaac Newton solved many difficult problems. But even he admitted that trying to explain the tides was the only problem that made his head ache. But he did finally solve the problem. After scientists read the *Principia*, no one seriously doubted Isaac Newton's explanation.

How large are average tides? The size of a tide is measured by how much the water rises from low tide to the following high tide.

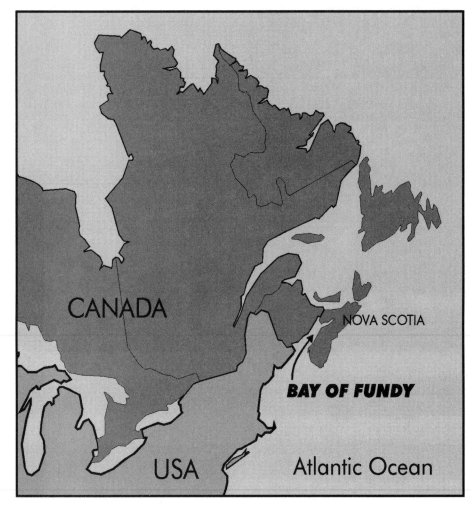

The Bay of Fundy has the world's greatest tidal range.

fishermen climbed ladders and plucked out the fish entangled in the nets ten feet in the air!

Usually tides work to man's advantage. The typical cargo ship needs 30 feet of water to float. Tides make the depth of even small rivers and bays safe to enter at certain times during the day. Rivers become important ports of trade.

Ocean tides offer a tremendous source of unused energy. A loaded cargo ship weighs as much as a skyscraper, but tides lift the ship as easily as they would a cork. Inventors have come up with many ingenious schemes to change the surging power of tides into energy.

Along the United States coastline the average is four feet. Out in the Pacific Ocean where there is no land to cause the water to pile up, tides are about two feet. Lake Michigan has tides of two inches.

The difference in size of a tide is caused by the land that it strikes. Some bays are long and sloping, with funnel-shaped shores. The shores tighten together and squeeze water into smaller bays.

In the Bay of Fundy the combined attraction of the sun and moon causes a drop from high tide to low tide of 70 feet.

At one time fishermen along the coast of Nova Scotia went fishing with stepladders. They hung nets on tall poles during low tide. When the tide turned, sea water carrying fish surged back into the bay from the Atlantic Ocean. Then, at the next low tide, the

The first successful attempts were by mill owners who trapped water at high tide in ponds. Then they released the water slowly to turn mill wheels to make grain into flour.

In Washington, DC, tides are used to clean out the reflecting pool of the Washington Monument. Each day at high tide water flows from the Potomac River into a lake called the Tidal Basin. At low tide water is released from the basin to sweep through the reflecting pool.

The only large-scale use of tidal power is on the Rance River in France where a long dam separates the river from the sea. Tides generate electricity both at high tide when water surges through the turbines, and at low tide when water escapes. The project generates enough energy to supply a city with a population of 100,000.

Questions

The Mystery of Tides

Choose A or B to complete the sentence.

1. The ancient Greeks
    - A. did not know about tides.
    - B. knew all about tides.

2. A Roman invasion of England failed because of the Romans' lack of experience with
    - A. the full moon.
    - B. tides.

3. Tables that predicted tides were often in error
    - A. because busy ports had no time for tides.
    - B. because of winds and weather conditions.

4. The first person to correctly explain the cause of tides was
    - A. Christopher Columbus.
    - B. Isaac Newton.

5. Isaac Newton's book, The *Principia*, is
    - A. a lost manuscript.
    - B. the most important science book ever published.

6. Isaac Newton had a passion for
    - A. Bible study.
    - B. raising flowers.

7. Tides are caused by the gravitational attraction of the moon and
    - A. the earth's core.
    - B. the sun.

Thought Questions:

8. Describe some of the reasons that predicting tides is difficult.

_____

_____

9. Describe some of the benefits of tides.

_____

_____

CHAPTER 9

THE COMPASS POINTS THE WAY

Successful navigation makes it possible for a ship to leave port and arrive at its destination safely. Often the voyage takes a ship out of sight of land. Under those conditions, three facts must be known: the ship's position, speed, and course.

The compass makes it possible for a navigator to set his course. The ability of a compass to point north seemed mysterious to most sailors. They didn't entirely understand it, and they certainly did not trust it.

Magnetism was known for centuries before it was put to use as a compass. The scientist who first wrote about magnets was Thales (THAY-leez) who lived about 600 B.C. He lived in the Greek province of Magnesia on the western coast of what is now Turkey. Deposits of an iron ore had been discovered in Magnesia. This ore, magnetite, would attract pieces of iron. It is, of course, from the province of Magnesia that magnetite, magnetic, and magnetism all received their names.

When Thales suspended a piece of magnetite by a string, it always pointed in a north-south direction. Because of this property, natural magnets became known as lodestone. The word lodestone means "leading stone."

Modern compass

Thales stroked an iron needle with the natural magnet. When he did, the iron needle became magnetized, too.

Not until the 1200s did Mediterranean sailors begin to use the magnetic compass for navigating. The early sailors didn't trust the compass, so they only relied upon it when they had no choice.

The first compasses were made simply by floating a magnetized needle upon a straw in a wooden bowl filled with water. The end of the needle that pointed north was called the north-seeking pole, or simply the north pole. The other end was the south-seeking pole, or simply the south pole.

The earth's magnetic poles are not fixed into position. They wander around from year to year. Sometimes they move by several hundred miles.

By the 1400s, this primitive compass had been replaced by a needle balanced on a pivot.

Sailors mistrusted the compass for the very good reason that the compass did on occasion lead them astray. Sometimes the sailors themselves caused the problem by putting iron objects too near the compass needle. The magnetic needle attracted the iron object, which pulled the needle off course.

But at other times, the compass did give misleading readings. What caused the problems?

William Gilbert, an English physician, investigated magnetism and wrote a book on the subject. His book, *Concerning Magnetism*, separated truth from fiction about the subject. He showed that unlike magnetic poles attract, while like magnetic poles repel each other. He also showed that the strength of a magnet grows weaker by the square of the distance. Suppose you move a magnet twice as close to an iron nail. The attraction is four times as great: $2 \times 2 = 4$; move it one-third as close and the attraction becomes nine times as great: $3 \times 3 = 9$.

People believed that a compass pointed north because the heavens above the earth's North Pole attracted it. Gilbert wanted to test this idea. But how could he?

William Gilbert constructed an unusual compass. The needle in his compass could dip up and down rather than left and right. He pointed the compass north and released the needle. Instead of pointing to the heavens, the needle dipped down by an angle of about 70°.

Why did the needle point down instead of up? William Gilbert concluded that compass needles do not point to the heavens. Instead, they point to magnetic poles of the earth. Gilbert's dip compass pointed to a magnetic pole thousands of miles away from London and below the horizon.

"The earth itself is a magnet," William Gilbert explained. "One pole is somewhere in the Arctic and the other pole is in the Antarctic."

The earth does act as a large magnet. A compass points north because the compass needle aligns with the magnetic field of the earth.

The dip of the needle is greater the further north an explorer travels. An explorer can find the north magnetic pole by carrying a dip compass. When it points straight down, then the explorer is standing at the north magnetic pole.

But aren't the geographic north pole and the magnetic north pole the same? No, they're not. The geographic north pole is on the axis about which the earth rotates. At the geographic north pole, the north star is directly overhead. Geographic north is considered "true" north.

Hundreds of years ago sailors navigated thousands of miles of open sea in the South Pacific using the stars and clouds as their guides. Certain types of clouds form over islands. They scanned the horizon for these clouds knowing they had a good chance of finding an island beneath them. The Hawaiian islands were the last of the islands to be discovered and populated in the vast Pacific ocean.

In Gilbert's time, a compass in London pointed 11° east of north. This showed that the earth's magnetic poles and earth's geographic poles do not fall at the same points.

The magnetic pole in the northern hemisphere is located in the Hudson Bay region in northern Canada. It's about 1,100 miles from the geographic north pole. The magnetic pole in the southern hemisphere is located between Antarctica and Australia, west of Ross Sea. It is about 1,200 miles from the south geographic pole.

A compass points to the earth's magnetic pole, not its geographic pole. The sailors were right in mistrusting a compass. A magnetic compass does not always point true north. At a point in the South Atlantic midway between Africa and South America, a compass points about 25° west of north. In the Bering Sea off the coast of Alaska, the compass reads 15° east of north. However, along an irregular line that passes along the coast of Florida, the compass does point true north.

The earth's magnetic field is vast, but it is also very weak. The magnetic field around a horseshoe magnet may be 2,000 times stronger than the intensity of the earth's magnetic field. Because of its weakness, earth's magnetic field is easily upset. It can change in strength and position.

The sun has storms on its surface. These storms, which cause sunspots and flares, shoot charged particles into space. These particles stream from the sun in all directions. As these charged particles wash over the earth, they cause violent changes in the

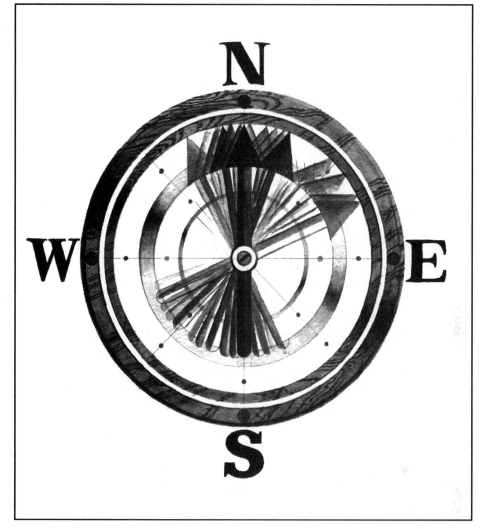

Compass readings are not 100 percent accurate. Several different factors cause the needle to change direction or to swing back and forth. Sunspots, mountain ranges, and the variations in the location of the magnetic poles all cause magnetic fluctuations.

earth's magnetic field. The magnetic storm sets off the northern lights. Radio communication becomes filled with static.

During a magnetic storm, compass readings undergo sudden, wild changes. Imagine how frightened seamen of the 1400s would become if the compass needle suddenly began swinging wildly.

The photo shows astronauts launching a satellite out of the space shuttle cargo bay.

The space age introduced a new way to know exactly where you are on the earth. With communication satellites in place, and if you have the right equipment you can find your location to within a few feet.

geographic north and magnetic north is called the magnetic declination. A London scientist in 1635 checked Gilbert's value for the magnetic declination. Instead of 11°, he found the declination to be 0°. Then as the years passed, it again read 11° as the north magnetic pole shifted back. Once, the declination in London went as high as 15°.

Because of the continuous shifting of the magnetic poles, navigation charts must be updated often.

Of course, until the 1600s, sailors didn't know all of these facts. But they did know that the compass sometimes acted up. It is no wonder that they hesitated to put their lives in the hands of a compass alone.

Minerals found in the earth's crust cause magnetic compasses to behave in unpredictable ways, too. Along the coast by mountain ranges, the compass needle is pulled off course. The effect is even greater on land, especially in the mountains. In certain regions in the Rocky Mountains, the north end of a compass actually points south.

The earth's magnetic poles are not fixed into position. They wander around from year to year. Sometimes they move by several hundred miles. The difference between

What causes the earth's magnetic field? Scientists don't know for certain even today. Many scientists suspect it may be caused by the flow of molten iron and nickel within the earth's core.

Today, navigation relies upon gyroscopic compasses. These devices contain a spinning wheel that also points in the same direction. Also, radio and satellite broadcasts make navigation much easier.

Questions

The Compass Points the Way

Choose A or B to complete the sentence.

1. Sailors sometimes caused their compasses to give false readings by
   - A. mounting them too high in the ship.
   - B. putting iron objects too near the compass needle.

2. The first person to separate truth from fiction about magnetism was
   - A. Benjamin Franklin.
   - B. William Gilbert.

3. The geographic north pole and the magnetic north pole fall
   - A. at the same place.
   - B. several hundred miles from one another.

4. The earth's magnetic field is vast
   - A. and very powerful.
   - B. but weak.

5. Particles shot from the sun during solar storms can cause
   - A. sudden changes in compass readings.
   - B. beautiful northern lights and nothing else.

Thought Question:

6. Describe how the dip compass proved that a compass needle points to the earth's magnetic poles rather than the heavens.

CHAPTER 10

TIME AND LONGITUDE

Any spot on land or sea can be located exactly only if both the latitude and longitude are known.

Latitude is the distance in degrees north or south of the equator. Lines of latitude are imaginary circles parallel to the equator. The circles of latitude are known as parallels.

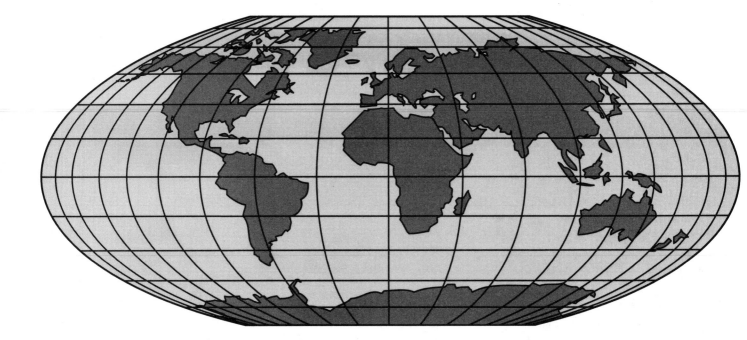

Lines of Latitude and Longitude divide the earth into a "grid" that allows exact navigation to take place.

Longitude lines measure distance east or west. They are imaginary circles of equal size which pass through both poles. Unlike latitude lines that are different sizes and never meet, the lines of longitude are all the same size and cross one another at the poles. The circles of longitude are known as meridians.

The equator is the reference line for latitude. It is an easy choice because it is the largest of the parallel circles going around the earth. As one travels toward the poles the parallels of latitude become smaller and smaller circles.

Latitude could be found easily enough, even by early explorers. Navigators on ships at sea found their approximate latitude by measuring the angle between the horizon and the sun or the North Star.

Meridians of longitude are all the same size. One of the meridians must be selected as the reference meridian. It is known as the prime meridian. The word *prime* is a Latin word meaning "first." All other meridians are counted from it.

The British measure longitude from a line that passes through the Royal Observatory in Greenwich, England. During the 1600s and 1700s, Great Britain was the most powerful sea-going nation in the world. It had the largest navy and the best ships. The British developed many of the tools of navigation. The British choice of the prime meridian was adopted by other countries as well.

Greenwich, England, on the prime meridian, has a longitude of 0 degrees. All other longitudes on earth are measured east or west of the prime meridian. St. Louis,

Galilei Galileo was a brilliant scientist born during a time of rigidly held beliefs. The leaders of the day believed certain things to be true and would not tolerate any "new" thinking. He was sentenced to house arrest from 1633 until his death in 1642.

Missouri, is located at 90 degrees west longitude. St. Louis is 90 degrees west of the prime meridian, one-fourth of the distance around the earth.

Finding the correct longitude is virtually impossible without an accurate clock.

How can a clock help a navigator find his longitude? The time of day is not the same everywhere on earth. Half of the earth is in

67

The Baptistry in front of The Cathedral in Florence, Italy, is a beautiful place to visit. It doesn't look much different than when Galileo was appointed court mathematician nearby in 1610 .

darkness. The other half is in daylight. When the sun is rising in one place on earth, it is setting halfway around the world. Elsewhere the time is midnight, or noon, or some other hour of the day.

Local time is the time of day at a particular place upon the earth. Local time can be found by observing the position of the sun or the stars.

Navigators can find their longitude by carrying an accurate clock with them that has been set to Greenwich time. If the local time agrees with the clock, then their ship is somewhere along the prime meridian. But elsewhere, the local time and Greenwich time will differ.

For instance, the difference between local time and Greenwich time in St. Louis, Missouri, is 6 hours. That means St. Louis is 90 degrees west of Greenwich. When the sun is directly overhead along the Greenwich meridian, it is just rising over St. Louis, Missouri.

From the difference between Greenwich time and local time, navigators can calculate longitude. The earth has 360 degrees and 24 hours. Each hour is 15 degrees. One hour of time equals 15 degrees of longitude.

But the clock must be accurate. If it loses 15 seconds each day, then at the end of a six month voyage the clock would be off by 45 minutes. At the equator, this would lead to an error in longitude of 50 miles.

The early navigators like Columbus and Magellan had no accurate clocks. Time and again explorers sighted islands and marked their location on maps. Later, when other ships tried to return, the islands couldn't be found. The islands hadn't vanished, of course. Instead, their real location had not been plotted accurately enough in the first place.

Navigators need an accurate clock that can be trusted to keep Greenwich time on board a rolling and pitching ship. The clock must keep accurate time for several months, despite the hardships of an ocean voyage.

The oldest method of measuring time was probably the sundial. It is certainly the oldest method of timekeeping for which we have a written record. In the Bible, in Isaiah 38:1-8 it describes how the sun was used to tell time.

Hezekiah, the king of Judah, became sick. Isaiah, the prophet, came to him and said he would die. However, Hezekiah prayed for longer life. God granted him another 15 years. As a sign of this He had the sun move backward:

> Behold, I will bring again the shadow of the degrees, which is gone down in the sun dial of Ahaz, ten degrees backward. So the sun returned ten degrees, by which degrees it was gone down (Isa. 38:8).

The most accurate of the ancient clocks was the Egyptian clepsydra, or water clock. The word clepsydra means "water thief." Water dripped into a container at a steady rate. The rising water raised a wooden

float. From its position the hour could be read.

Although the water clock was the best of the ancient timepieces, it had serious drawbacks. It could only keep time to the nearest 15 minutes or so. Not only was it inaccurate, but on a cold night the water froze and the clock stopped.

Sundials were used for judging time before clocks and watches became more available in the 18th century.

Dry sand can be used instead of water. It measures time by the fall of sand through a narrow opening. Sand trickles from one glass bulb into a second bulb. Sand glasses can measure short intervals of time — from a few seconds to an hour. During the Middle Ages, some churches used sand glasses to limit the length of sermons.

Sand glasses aided navigators in estimating the speed of ships. The navigator threw a log overboard. Attached to it was a rope with knots in it at regular distances. The motion of the ship left the log behind and pulled out the rope. The navigator counted the number of knots that passed through his hands in a given interval of time. This interval of time, usually 28 seconds, was measured with a sand glass. The speed of the ship was given in "knots," a term still used to describe the speed of a ship. The captain recorded information in a "log" book, a reference to the log thrown overboard to measure speed.

In the Middle Ages, the first mechanical clocks were installed in

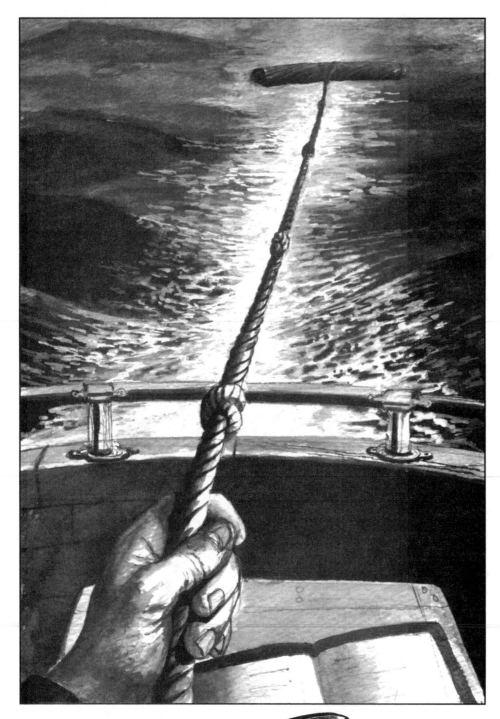

Speed is measured by time and distance. To measure the speed of a ship, a navigator tossed a log overboard with a rope attached. The rope had knots at regular intervals. By counting the knots that passed through his hands in a given period of time, the navigator could calculate the ship's speed.

churches and city halls. Falling weights, rather than dripping water, drove these clocks. A rope attached to the falling weight uncoiled and turned a drum. These mechanical clocks were bulky giants that weighed several tons.

Most had only an hour hand. Putting a minute hand on them would be worthless. Some had no hands at all. Instead, they rang a bell every hour. The word "clock" is from a French word for "bell."

None of the clocks at the time of Columbus could withstand the rigors of an ocean voyage. They could not keep accurate time from one day to the next, much less for the several months of an ocean voyage. The only timekeeper that Columbus had on his voyage was a sand glass.

The story of accurate clocks begins with Galileo and his discovery of the principle of the pendulum. Galileo was born the year Michelangelo died, 1564, and died the year Isaac Newton was born, 1642.

Galileo was born in Pisa, near Florence, in Italy. His father, Vincenzio Galileo, was a musician. He made barely enough money from his profession to support his family. He

To an observant person even something as simple as a swinging candle can lead to amazing discoveries.

insisted that Galileo attend college to study medicine. Doctors commanded respect and made good money.

Galileo himself liked the idea of college. But he did not like the way medicine was taught at the University of Pisa where he attended. The professors sat on raised platforms at the front of the room. They lectured by reading from the books of ancient Greek scholars. They ignored the discoveries of modern scientists.

Galileo believed that the future of science lay in experiments. He made his first important discovery as a teenager while a medical student. The students attended chapel service each morning. Contrary to the false charges of heresy later brought against him by jealous professors, Galileo was always a pious man.

One morning in 1581, Galileo knelt and whispered his prayers in the dark chapel. He arose to watch a lamplighter light the candles in lamps hanging 30 feet from the high ceiling. The hanging lamps had small cords attached to them so they could be pulled to the balcony to be lighted.

Lighting the candles caused the lamps to swing in a slow back and forth motion that slowly died down. To Galileo, it seemed that the time of the swing was the same, whether the lamp swung in a wide arc or swung in a barely noticeable arc. He tested this by timing the lamp's swing with his pulse. The lamp took no longer to make a giant swing than it did to make a short one.

He returned to his room to try other experiments with pendulums. A pendulum is any object free to swing in a back and forth motion. Galileo made a pendulum by hanging a weight to the end of a string. He pulled the weight, called a bob to one side, and let it go.

Only by lengthening or shortening the string could he change the time for a complete swing. When the string is short the pendulum swings more briskly. When it is long, the pendulum swings more leisurely. A pendulum that is 9-3/4 inches (24.8 cm) long will have a period of one second.

Pendulum

The pendulum is an accurate way of marking off equal intervals of time. Galileo's discovery of the principle of the pendulum would eventually lead to the invention of an accurate clock.

The first person to make such a pendulum clock was Christiaan Huygens (HOY-genz), the son of an official in the Dutch government. Christiaan Huygens received a good education at the University of Leiden. He became a telescope maker and invented an improved telescope. In 1656, he discovered Titan, the largest moon of Saturn. A year later he saw the rings of Saturn and described their true nature.

Astronomy led Christiaan Huygens to an interest in time keeping. Eclipses of the sun and moon, the position of the planets, and all of the other events in the sky can only be predicted if time is measured precisely,

In 1656, about a dozen years after Galileo died, Huygens devised a way to hook a pendulum to the gears of a clock. The regular back and forth motion of the pendulum ticked off exact intervals of time. Falling weights gave just enough motion to the pendulum to keep it moving against friction and air resistance.

As the ability to navigate became more of an exact science, mapmaking became more precise and reliable. Ships could now meet in the middle of the great oceans with certainty. Sailors that lived before reliable navigational tools were developed preferred to keep land in sight.

Huygens invented the grandfather clock, the first truly accurate clock. It was precise enough for scientific purposes.

His fame spread throughout Europe. Huygens moved to Paris, France. In Paris he helped organize the French Academy of Sciences. He patterned that organization after the Royal Society in England.

A few years later, the king of France began a series of religious persecutions. Because of his Christian beliefs, Huygens was forced to leave Paris. He returned to the Netherlands where he could worship freely.

Despite the great accuracy of Huygen's clock, it could not be used aboard a ship.

The tossing about by waves upset the pendulum.

What navigators needed was a *chronometer*, an extremely accurate clock to determine longitude at sea. The word chronometer is from two Greek words, *chrono* and *meter* meaning "time measure."

In 1713 the British government offered a prize of 20,000 pounds for an accurate ship's clock. The prize was worth more than an average worker would earn in a lifetime. The British Parliament assumed the chronometer would be invented by a famous scientist who belonged to the Royal Society.

A self-trained mechanic named John Harrison of Yorkshire heard about the prize. In 1728 he began building a trustworthy chronometer. The first one took seven years to make. It weighed 72 pounds. It kept good time, but in making it he learned more about clock making. He finished a second clock in 1739. It was even larger and weighed 103 pounds.

Harrison started the next clock even before he completely tested the second one. For 17 years John Harrison labored over his "Number Three." During this time he received small sums of money from the British government to keep up the work. Harrison completed Number Three in 1757.

The first three clocks were big and heavy, and they looked clumsy. But he'd learned many tricks in making them. He knew he could make a more compact clock.

In only two years he turned out Number Four. It was a triumph of instrument making. Number Four was only five inches in diameter and an inch thick. He enclosed it in a brushed metal case, and made the hands of lacquered colors. The clock succeeded as a timekeeper of unsurpassed performance. It also succeeded as a work of art. Seldom had a clock looked so beautiful.

Finally, 33 years after he began, John Harrison put Number Four aboard a ship sailing to Jamaica. It proved itself in all respects. It was more accurate at sea than any other clock at that time on land. It was off by less than a minute after five months aboard ship.

Harrison's design should have won Parliament's prize. For some reason the government officials declared the test as "not conclusive." Parliament repeatedly made demands for changes. John Harrison met every demand. Still, they refused to give him the prize.

Finally, it became clear that those in charge were stalling. They hoped that some of their friends would win the prize. It wouldn't do for some lowly mechanic from Yorkshire to succeed when gentlemen scientists of the Royal Society had failed.

John Harrison took his case to the people. He wrote a pamphlet telling about how he'd been treated. King George III petitioned Parliament on Harrison's behalf. Bowing under public opinion, Parliament at last paid John Harrison the 20,000 pounds. He received the reward in 1772 after 44 years of work.

Harrison's chronometer was a milestone in navigation. It allowed sailors to calculate longitude on the open ocean. For the first time ships could meet at appointed times in mid-ocean to exchange mail and supplies. Tiny islands could be located with precision in the vast Pacific.

Captain William Bligh carried a duplicate of Harrison's Number Four chronometer aboard the ill-fated *Bounty*. That voyage ended in a mutiny led by Fletcher Christian in 1789. The mutineers took Number Four. Eventually the clock found its way back to London where it is still in existence.

Questions

Time and Longitude

Supply the missing number.

1. The longitude of a point on the prime meridian.

2. The number of hours in a day.

3. The number of degrees in a complete circle.

4. In Isaiah 38:8, the number of degrees the sun moved backward.

Match the person in one column with the correct choice in the other column:

5. Hezekiah   a. carried a copy of Number Four on the *Bounty.*

6. Christopher Columbus   b. discovered the principle of the pendulum.

7. Galileo   c. had no accurate clock on his voyages.

8. Christian Huygens   d. made the first accurate clock for sea voyages.

9. John Harrison   e. made the first pendulum clock.

10. William Bligh   f. prayed for longer life.

Thought Question:

11. Explain the difference between local time and Greenwich time.

_____

_____

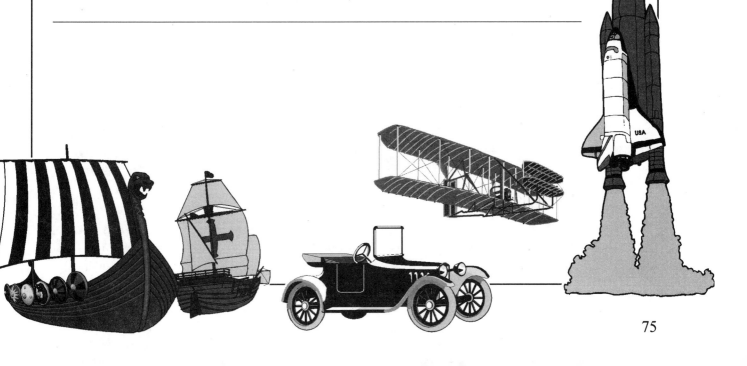

CHAPTER 11

A RIVER IN THE OCEAN

The waters of the oceans are in constant motion. Both Columbus and Magellan experienced ocean currents, although they didn't recognize their importance.

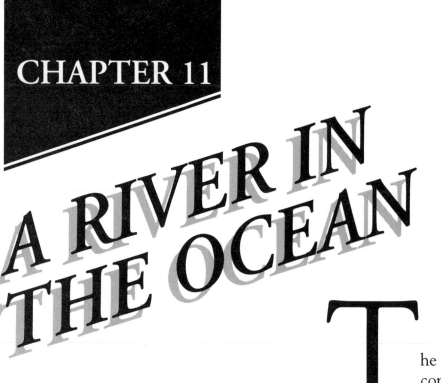

This map of the Atlantic Ocean was created in the year 1513, just 21 years after Christopher Columbus made his first voyage to the new world.

Prevailing winds and favorable currents carried Columbus westward from Spain. When his ships started home, they battled winds and currents. Columbus found it impossible to retrace exactly his course. Instead, he sailed north. There he found a west wind and a current flowing generally toward Europe.

Detailed charts of ocean currents would enable sea captains to make ocean voyages more quickly and in greater safety. But such charts didn't exist until well into the 1800s. The person who traced out ocean currents was Matthew Maury, an American naval officer.

Matthew Maury grew up on a Virginia farm. While still in his teens, he left the farm and entered the navy as midshipman. He spent the next four years on a cruise that took him around the world.

He trained for the time he would command his own ship. These plans changed in 1839 when a stagecoach accident left him permanently lamed. The physical disability made it impossible for him to command a ship. He retired from active duty.

The Navy gave him a sinecure. The word *sinecure* means "without care." People given sinecures are paid a salary, but do not have to report to anyone. The military gave such jobs as a reward to faithful employees who had become disabled and couldn't earn a living any other way. People who received sinecures were not expected to work.

In Maury's case he was put in charge of the Depot of Charts and Instruments. It was a job with no duties. But Matthew Maury refused to take the government's money without working. He collected charts and navigation instruments. Eventually, his office became the United States Naval Observatory.

He threw himself into the study of the ocean. He collected log books from United States naval and merchant ships. He studied their daily observations. His goal was to

Matthew Maury is considered to be the father of oceanography. He spent many years making wind and current charts of the Atlantic, Pacific, and Indian Oceans.

prepare charts that showed the speed and direction of ocean currents.

Most people believed ocean currents were broad and ill-defined. "Currents in the sea aren't reliable. They come and go. You're wasting your time."

Matthew Maury read in the Bible in Psalm 8 that there are paths in the sea. He believed if the Bible said there were paths in the sea, then he could find them and map them.

Benjamin Franklin helped write the Declaration of Independence and was one of its signers.

Matthew Maury discovered that Benjamin Franklin had investigated an ocean current known as the Gulf Stream. In the 1760s Franklin served as Postmaster General for the Colonies. British captains operated mail packets between England and the Colonies. The packet ships had been specially designed for speed. Yet, they made very slow progress across the Atlantic. They failed to deliver mail on time. Colonists complained to Franklin about the slow mail service.

Benjamin Franklin investigated. He learned that American whaling vessels from the colonies often crossed the Atlantic faster than the British packets. How could a slow, lumbering whaling ship outrun a speedy packet?

Benjamin Franklin spoke to a captain of whaling ships. "Why does your ship do so much better than the British packets?"

"We are well-acquainted with the Gulf Stream, and the British are not," the captain explained. "We informed them that they were fighting a current that was against them. When the winds are light, the current cancels their western travel. And when the winds are good they still lose 70 miles a day. We told them about the current. They were too 'wise' to learn from simple American fishermen. They ignored our advice."

Benjamin Franklin thought a map could be drawn showing the position of the Gulf Stream. But he never succeeded in doing so.

Matthew Maury tried to trace the route of the Gulf Stream. He distributed especially prepared logbooks to captains of American vessels. Although the log books helped, his map of the Gulf Stream remained mostly blank. Despite Maury's best efforts there was too much ocean and too few naval vessels.

"Good navigation charts call for the combined action of several countries," Matthew Maury decided. He planned an international meeting and invited people from all over to attend. The meeting took place in 1853 in Brussels, Belgium. It marked one of the great steps forward for the study of the oceans.

Slowly, the path of the Gulf Stream took shape. It had a definite width, depth, and direction.

"There is a river in the sea," Maury said in describing the Gulf Stream. "In the severest droughts it never fails, and in the mightiest floods it never overflows. Its banks and its bottom are of cold water, while its current is of warm. The Gulf of Mexico is its fountain, and its mouth is in the Arctic seas. It is the Gulf Stream.

"There is in the world no other such majestic flow of waters. Its current is more rapid than the Mississippi or Amazon, and its volume more than a thousand times greater."

The waters of the Gulf Stream are an indigo blue. The line between the Gulf Stream and the regular ocean water is very distinct. Often one-half of a ship may be seen floating in the dark blue of the Gulf Stream water, while the other half is in the green of common sea water.

The rivers in the sea are the biggest moving things on earth. The Gulf Stream is a much larger river than any on land. It is 50 miles wide at the start, nearly a half mile deep, and moves at speeds up to four miles an hour.

Although prevailing winds and the spin of the earth play a role in causing ocean currents, they are not the main cause. The single most important factor in giving ocean currents their life are temperature differences.

Ocean currents *are* like vast rivers. They have no river banks to guide them. Instead, they are held in place by temperature differences.

Surface water is cooled in polar regions. Cold water sinks. As the cold polar water sinks, warm water from the equator flows out to take its place.

The deep water near the ocean floor is only a degree or two above freezing. Even in the tropics, the sun's rays are unable to penetrate deeper than 600 feet or so.

Warm surface currents, like the Gulf Stream in the Atlantic, flow toward the poles. They are narrow and fast. Cold currents, like the Humboldt in the Pacific, flow toward the equator. They are wide and slow.

This circulation is essential to sea life. Sea water at the surface picks up oxygen. Water becomes stagnant and lifeless without oxygen. Currents carry oxygen rich water into the deepest trenches.

The Gulf Stream is a river in the Atlantic Ocean.

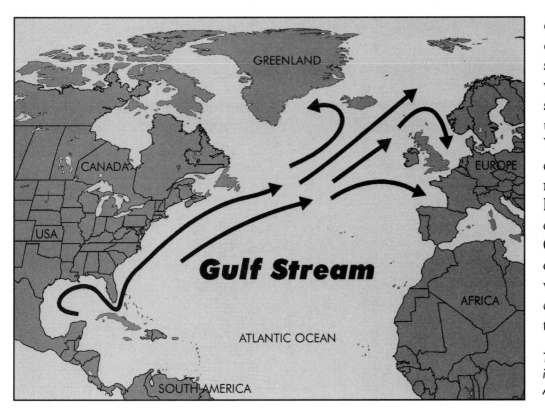

GREENLAND

CANADA

USA

Gulf Stream

EUROPE

AFRICA

ATLANTIC OCEAN

SOUTH AMERICA

Shrimp-like creatures have been found in the Marianas Trench. It's the deepest part of the ocean.

In 1844, Samuel F. B. Morse gave his successful demonstration of the telegraph. Within a few years that new invention had proven its worth. Telegraph lines linked all the important cities along the eastern seaboard of the United States.

Businessmen with imagination began to draw up plans to lay a submerged cable from the United States to Europe.

The Atlantic Cable Company asked Matthew Maury to help. They asked him to make a chart of the Atlantic, not of the surface, but of the ocean floor. He would chose the best route along the sea bottom to lay the telegraph cable.

The Atlantic cable took 15 years. The work was interrupted by storms, breaks in the cable, lack of money, and the Civil War. But the cable did eventually succeed.

In the process Maury began step by step exploration of the sea bottom. He made maps of the oceans that went beyond showing islands and other features. He explored the properties of the sea, not only on its surface, but throughout its depths.

In 1855 he published the first textbook about the ocean. *Physical Geography of the Sea* became the breakthrough book in oceanography. His book was extremely successful. Matthew Maury made it clear in the book that he believed the Bible to be accurate when it touched upon scientific subjects.

The Navy raised Matthew Maury to the rank of commander. To the American people he earned another title, a more important one, as "The Pathfinder of the Seas."

The American Civil War broke out in 1861. Matthew Maury followed his home state — Virginia — out of the Union. He became head of coast, harbor, and river defenses for the Confederacy. He was sent on missions to England for supplies. He repeatedly sailed through the northern naval blockades.

After the Civil War, with the South defeated, Matthew Maury believed he would not be welcome in the United States. For a time he lived in Mexico.

In only two years, however, his native country asked him to return. He became a professor of meteorology at the Virginia Military Institute.

Meteorology is the study of weather. Oceanology and weather are related to one another. Weathermen have found that weather is greatly affected by the temperature, size and direction of ocean currents. Many land areas of the world owe their climates to the currents in the sea.

The Gulf Stream carries warm water. This makes a profound change in the weather around the Atlantic. It warms the British Isles. England would be bitterly cold without the warmth of the Gulf Stream.

A desert lies along much of the west coast of South America because of the Humboldt current. California and Florida would be much hotter if currents off the shore did not siphon off extra amounts of heat.

In 1868, Matthew Maury settled in Lexington, Virginia. There he lived his last years in peace.

The United States honored him for his great achievements. The Naval Academy at Annapolis named Maury Hall in his honor. He was elected to the Hall of Fame for Great Americans in 1930.

On his tombstone at the United States Naval Academy is inscribed Psalm 8. Verse eight of that Psalm reads, ". . . whatsoever passeth through the paths of the seas."

Questions

A River in the Ocean

Choose A or B to complete the sentence.

1. People who received sinecures were
   - A. given command of the best ships.
   - B. not expected to work.

2. The first person who tried to trace out the Gulf Stream was
   - A. Benjamin Franklin.
   - B. English mail ships.

3. The statement "there is a river in the sea" refers to
   - A. the Gulf Stream.
   - B. a mythical place near Atlantis.

4. The primary factor in giving ocean currents their life is
   - A. migration of whales.
   - B. temperature differences.

5. Matthew Maury's tombstone has on it a quote from
   - A. his book.
   - B. the Bible.

Thought Questions:

6. Why did captains of British mail ships not listen to the captains of American whaling vessels?
   _____
   _____

7. Describe some of the effects of ocean currents upon sea life and climate.
   _____
   _____

CHAPTER 12

THREE SPHERES

Scientists think of the earth as made of three shells or spheres. Each sphere is inside the other, like the layers of an onion. Each sphere corresponds to one of the three states of matter: lithosphere (solid), hydrosphere (liquid), and atmosphere (gas).

The *lithosphere* includes all the solid surface of the earth and everything inside it. *Litho* is a Greek word meaning "stone." When scientists examine the solid earth underfoot, almost all the material is rock. Sand, gravel, soil, and vegetation may form a thin surface layer, but bedrock is always found to be under this loose cover.

The earth is unique among planets. It could be called the water planet. Genesis chapter one tells the story of God's creation of earth.

Scientists can directly explore only a tiny part of the lithosphere. The deepest mines have shafts two miles deep. The deepest wells drilled in search of gas and oil are five miles deep. Volcanic eruptions bring up rocky material from as deep as 20 miles. Explorers can't go very far into the earth. The pressure and temperature there are much too high. Instead, they explore from a distance by remote means.

Scientists probe the inside of the earth by shock waves caused by earthquakes and man-made explosions. How the waves behave depends upon the material through which they pass. As waves pass from one layer into another, they change direction and speed.

Scientists have built a model of the inside of the earth based on their study of earthquake waves. This model divides the lithosphere into three layers: crust, mantle, and core.

At the center of the earth is the core with a radius of about 2,200 miles. The exact nature of material at the core of the earth is difficult to predict from earthquake waves alone. But the core of the earth is believed to be made mostly of iron and nickel.

Above the core is the second division of the lithosphere, an 1800-mile thick layer of rock called called the mantle. The material of the mantle has never been seen either. Earthquake waves indicate that it is probably

Cutaway of the earth's interior and the first two layers of the atmosphere.

made of minerals that are rich in metals like iron and magnesium.

The crust is the part of the lithosphere that scientists know the best. Like the shell of an egg, the crust is the outermost and thinnest shell. It covers the earth like the skin of a very slightly wrinkled apple. It is difficult to think of the Himalaya mountain

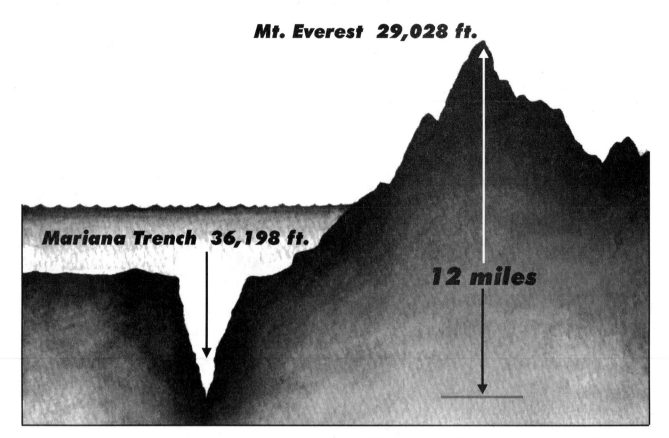

Mt. Everest 29,028 ft.

Mariana Trench 36,198 ft.

12 miles

Even though Mt. Everest and the Mariana Trench are thousands of miles apart the above illustration shows the greatest surface differences in the earth's crust.

range as a slight "wrinkle" in the crust of the earth, but it is, nonetheless. The maximum change in elevation in the surface of the earth is from the Marianas Trench at the bottom of the Pacific to the top of Mt. Everest. This distance is about 65,000 feet — about 12 miles.

If the earth were reduced to the size of a basketball, the greatest unevenness in its surface would be only 1/50 of an inch. Earth's rugged terrain is actually very smooth. It is far smoother than the surface of a basketball if both were the same size.

The rotation of the earth causes a slight flattening at the poles and a bulge at the equator. This bulge is about the same as the distance from the deepest trench to the top of Mt. Everest. A person at the equator is farther from the center of the earth than he would be at the top of Mt. Everest.

The crust and mantle do not blend into one another. Instead, there is a sharp change from the brittle crust and the mantle. The boundary is called the Moho discontinuity. A sudden change in properties is called a discontinuity. The Moho discontinuity is named in honor of Andrija Mohorovicic (moh-ho-ro-VEE-cheech), a Yugoslav geologist who discovered it in 1909.

Mohorovicic found that earthquake waves that went deeper in the earth arrived sooner than waves traveling along the surface. Earthquake waves travel at different speeds depending upon the material though which they pass. The Moho discontinuity shows that there is a sharp difference between the material that makes up the mantle and the crust.

The boundary between crust and mantle is nearest the surface under the deep oceans. In certain spots, the mantle may be only three miles under the crust. During the 1960s, scientists began a project for boring through the crust and into the mantle. They chose a place in the ocean near Hawaii where the crust was especially thin. The drilling equipment was designed, but *Project Moho* was abandoned because it cost too much.

It is strange to think that scientists have studied moon rocks from 240,000 miles away, but not earth material from less than 40 miles underground.

The *hydrosphere* is the liquid part of the earth. *Hydro* is a Greek word meaning "water." The hydrosphere covers almost three-fourths of the earth's surface, with the oceans making the greatest part of it by far.

Here at the Grand Canyon (Hopi Point), Arizona you can see a gash a mile deep in the earth's surface.

It includes not only oceans, lakes, and rivers, but also ice, snow, and water vapor in clouds.

In fact, the name *earth* is misleading. Our planet could well be called *water*. From space, the planet is a misty ball of blue-green oceans, brilliant white ice sheets, and clouds of water vapor. During winter as much as 20 percent of the earth's land area is covered by snow, another form of water.

The earth is unusual among the planets of the solar system in that water can exist in all three states — as a solid such as snow and ice; as a liquid in rivers and lakes and oceans; and as a gas in water vapor. The earth orbits the right distance from the sun. Any farther and the earth's water would be frozen solid. Any closer and it would all boil away.

The earth is the only body in the solar system, as far as we know, to have oceans.

The largest single body of water on earth is the Pacific Ocean. Turn a globe of the earth until the Pacific Ocean faces you. What you see is water. Except for a few islands and bits of land around the edge, the Pacific Ocean is a giant circular sea that covers half of the earth. It is the largest and deepest ocean — 10,000 miles across and a maximum of 7 miles deep.

The Pacific Ocean covers about 49 percent of the earth's surface and contains about 52 percent of the earth's water. In other words, a little more than half of all the water on earth is found in the Pacific Ocean.

The other oceans (Atlantic and Indian and various bays and seas that connect to them) make up another 46 percent of all the water on earth.

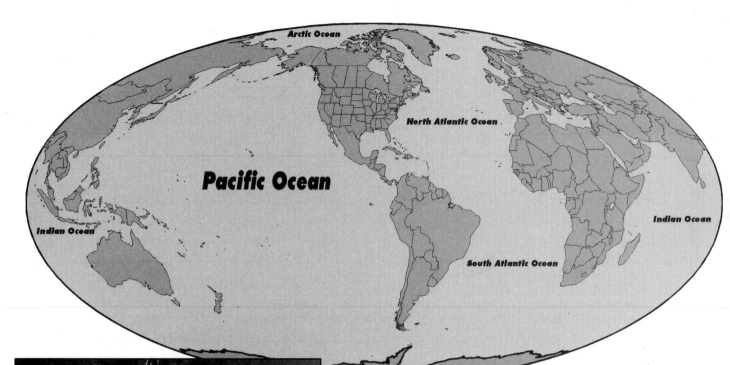

Arctic Ocean

North Atlantic Ocean

Pacific Ocean

Indian Ocean

Indian Ocean

South Atlantic Ocean

The Pacific ocean is not only the world's largest and deepest ocean, but it is one of many contrasts: from tropical islands near the equator (left), to the frozen north and south poles with their frozen interiors and glaciers that give birth to icebergs (below). The continents around the rim of the Pacific basin have a lot of earthquakes and there are many active volcanos. All this geologic activity has given the area the name "ring of fire."

The average ocean depth is 12,400 feet, a little over two miles. The maximum ocean depth is 37,730 feet in the Marianas Trench southwest of Guam in the Pacific. The bottom of the sea is absolutely dark since sunlight doesn't penetrate more than about 600 feet.

The pressure increases steadily at the rate of 14.7 pounds per square inch for every 34 feet in depth. At the ocean floor the water pressure reaches several tons per square inch. In many ways, it is easier for people to walk on the moon than to explore the ocean floor only two or three miles away.

Divers descend about 200 feet at most. Submarines can do a little better, to about 600 feet.

To go even deeper, William Beebe, an American naturalist, developed the bathysphere. The word *bathysphere* means "deep sphere." It is a steel chamber in the shape of a sphere. Porthole windows are made of thick quartz to withstand the crushing pressure deep in the ocean.

In the 1930s William Beebe made deep sea diving expeditions to a depth of over 3,000 feet. A ship on the surface lowered the steel sphere into the sea.

In all, Beebe made 30 dives. But the bathysphere had the disadvantage and danger of being held by a cable lowering it from a surface ship. It could not move around either.

The most successful exploration ship is a *bathyscaphe*. The word bathyscaphe means "deep ship." It was invented by August Piccard (pee-KAHR), a Swiss scientist. The bathyscaphe can be steered about, and it is not connected to a surface ship by cable.

In many ways, a bathyscaphe is like a dirigible blimp. The blimp gains lift by the balloon of light gases. In the bathyscaphe, a tank contains gasoline to give the vessel lift. Gasoline floats in water. A load of metal shot causes the bathyscaphe to sink. By releasing the metal shot, the bathyscaphe rises to the surface. Below the tank is a steel sphere which contains the human explorers.

The deepest dive on record was carried out by Jacques Piccard (August's son) and Don Walsh who descended in 1960 by bathyscaphe to the bottom of the Marianas Trench. Since this is the deepest point in the ocean, their record still stands today.

Explorers are learning how to use robot submarines to explore the ocean floor. These robot machines carry lights, cameras, and sonar equipment. Humans have learned how to take their spirit of adventure, their eyes and ears, to the ocean floor, but leave their bodies safe on land.

The *atmosphere* is the earth's third sphere. It contains the mixture of gases that we breathe. The atmosphere and the people who explored it will be taken up in later chapters.

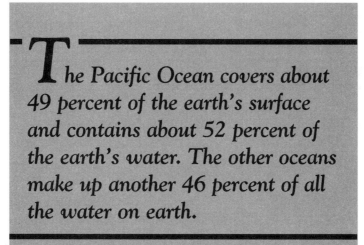

The Pacific Ocean covers about 49 percent of the earth's surface and contains about 52 percent of the earth's water. The other oceans make up another 46 percent of all the water on earth.

The Three Spheres

When God created the earth He knew exactly what kind of a planet we would need to survive. He knew we would need water, air to breath, and the earth under us.

At the Grand Canyon, Arizona, you can see deeper into the crust of the earth than anywhere else. Below you see a surfer enjoying the challenge of a big wave in Hawaii, and a mountain climber checking out the clouds as he rests on a mountain on Baffin Island, Canada, above the Arctic Circle.

Questions

Three Spheres

Match the item in the first column with the correct choice in the second column.

1. litho   a. deepest point in the ocean

2. hydro   b. dividing line between mantle and crust

3. atmosphere   c. prefix meaning "stone"

4. Himalayas mountain range   d. prefix meaning "water"

5. Moho discontinuity e. the sphere of gas

6. bathysphere   f. William Beebe's ship for deep sea diving

7. Marianas Trench   g. a wrinkle in the crust of the earth

Thought Question:

8. Describe some of the ways scientists explore the solid part of the earth.

_____

_____

9. Describe how gasoline and iron pellets cause Piccard's ship to sink and rise.

_____

_____

CHAPTER 13

INTO THE HEART OF THE GLACIER

The earth has a vast storehouse of ice. The Antarctic is covered by a slab of ice 10,000 feet thick. Greenland, too, is almost entirely covered by ice a mile thick. Most of the rocky surface of Greenland may actually be under sea level.

This glacial ice is the purest form of water found anywhere. It is so pure and so plentiful some scientists have proposed the use of tug boats to tow icebergs to countries short of fresh water.

Ancient people in warm climates seldom saw icebergs or glaciers. Ice to them seemed much more mysterious than it does to us today. The ancient Greeks saw ice

A glacier near Stewart Park, British Columbia looks like a river.

An early frost coats a Saint Anne's Lace flower. Below, frost crystals "grow" on a window pane in beautiful patterns.

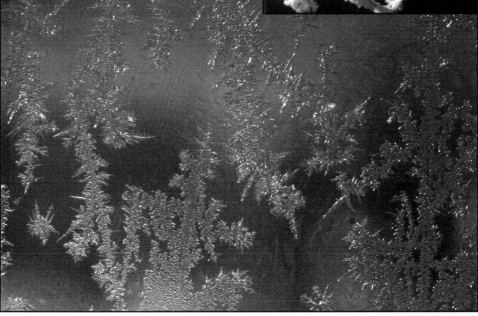

in the form of frost. Their word for frost is *kryllos* from which comes the English word "crystal," meaning clear. Water in thin sheets is perfectly clear. Clear substances were quite unusual before the invention of glass.

A *glacier* is a large body of permanent ice on land. Scientists believe glaciers are made by the accumulation of snowflakes. As the snow gets deeper, its weight compresses snow at lower levels. The snow turns to ice. A glacier may move down a slope by gravity, or spread outward in all directions because of

its own thickness. The earth's permanent ice covers about 10 percent of the earth's land area. Glaciers vary in size. Some of the glaciers in Glacier National Park, Montana, are less than a mile across. The Antarctica ice cap, with a size of almost five million square miles, is as big as a continent.

The ice cap at the South Pole covers the entire Antarctic continent. Its average thickness is 1.5 miles, but it may be 3.1 miles thick in places. About 86 percent of all the ice on earth is contained in the Antarctic glacier.

Another 10 percent of the total glacial ice covers most of Greenland. The remaining four percent is made up of small glaciers in Iceland, Alaska, and along mountain ranges around the world. Glaciers of one size or another are found on all the continents except Australia.

Lakes fed by water from melting glaciers can be instantly recognized. They have a beautiful emerald green color. The color is caused by particles of stone suspended in the water. The particles of stone, which are as fine as flour, are ground down by the action of the glacier.

Louis Agassiz was the first person to explore glaciers and learn that they can move. Louis Agassiz was born in Switzerland in 1807, the son of a simple Swiss preacher.

As a youngster, Louis studied birds, fish, snakes, frogs, and flowers. Yet he felt he had only gained a glimpse into the wonders of God's creation. He wanted to do so much more.

If only he could study science at the university. But only the rich could afford science. Who would pay a man to collect rocks and study the scales of fish?

"I believe God has given me the ability to study nature because that's what he wants me to do," Louis Agassiz said to his father.

Louis Agassiz's entire family made sacrifices so he could attend the University of Heidelberg, one of the best schools of Europe.

His active mind turned to two other things which made Switzerland famous: its glaciers and fossils.

In Switzerland during the 1830s, scientists found fossils everywhere. Fossils are skeletons or other remains left in stone by things that lived long ago.

For a time Louis worked with Georges Cuvier, a great French scientist who found many fossils. The great number of fossils

Louis Agassiz, a Swiss naturalist, traveled to Brazil and headed a zoological expedition in 1865, and sailed around Cape Horn to California in 1871.
He never tired of adventure in God's world.

bothered scientists because they could not explain why fossils should be so common.

Professor Cuvier said, "I believe that long ago a series of worldwide disasters came upon the earth. The last disaster was the great flood at the time of Noah, described in the Bible."

Like Professor Cuvier, Louis was devoted to the Word of God. He believed the great Flood described in Genesis caused many animals to be buried in mud and turned into fossils.

Louis Agassiz set to work with enthusiasm at the task of scraping away the stone from the delicate fossil skeletons. He found 340 types of fossil fish never known before. He filled five books with detailed drawings and interesting descriptions of the fishes he found. His books did more than describe the fishes. He made the ancient seas in which they swam come alive in the minds of readers.

Louis Agassiz earned a medical degree — Doctor Agassiz. Instead of practicing medicine, he moved to Neuchatel in Switzerland. There he could be near the glaciers he wanted to explore.

Some of the local people claimed that glaciers actually moved from year to year, like slow-moving rivers of ice. Most scientists did not believe that hard, frozen ice could flow.

Louis outfitted an expedition to study the glaciers up close.

He scrambled across the slippery fields of ice. Swirling snow made climbing unbearably cold and dangerous. Even in good weather sunlight melted snow, which loosened huge boulders which tumbled down the glacier.

Along the valley wall, Louis found deep scratches. He ran his finger along the deep cut. *What could have caused these scratches?* he wondered.

Then he hit upon the answer. Glaciers did move, and they pressed fallen boulders against the valley wall with force enough to cut deep grooves in the solid rock.

Louis found grooves like these all over Europe. Some time in the past the icy hand of glaciers had pushed their way south into warm climates. The glaciers would explain another puzzle.

Gigantic boulders dotted southern plains, far from the mountains.

"Glaciers carried the giant stones to their present locations and dropped them there when warmer weather melted the ice," Louis explained.

In his mind he could see the great river of ice — two miles thick — grinding down from the high Alps. It moved very slowly, of course, probably only a few feet each year. It wore down entire mountain ranges, cut out valleys, uprooted trees, and scraped away loose soil down to bedrock.

In 1837, Louis Agassiz spoke before a gathering of scientists. World famous men traveled from Paris, Berlin, Frankfurt, and London. Even Europe's most famous scientist, Baron von Humboldt, came.

Louis tacked up a map of the world on the wall. On it he had colored in the area covered by the Ice Age. When the men

Louis Agassiz looked upon his success as only seeing the order put in the universe by the Creator. He found in nature a constant reminder of God. "God writes the books of nature," Louis said. "I am only His librarian."

High in the Swiss Alps the Gornergott Glacier winds its way down to lower elevations.

realized what Louis was going to speak about, their faces tightened with disapproval.

Louis said, "Many years ago a long winter settled over a land previously covered with rich vegetation, where great beasts like those found in India and Africa freely roamed.

"Death entered with its terrors. With one blow of its violent hand it destroyed a mighty creation and wrapped all nature in a shroud of ice."

A German scientist scowled. "Moving glaciers? Never! Ice stays in the Alps. It does not travel anywhere else."

A French scientist said, "Earth's climate doesn't change from year to year. Worldwide disasters can't occur."

Louis said, "Not only do glaciers move, but in the past they reached as far south as the Mediterranean Sea."

After the speech, Alexander von Humboldt spoke privately to Louis Agassiz. "Protect your scientific reputation," he cautioned. "Leave your icy researches alone."

Louis went back to the Aar Glacier. He built a simple shelter on the ice. It had a blanket for a door and an overhanging ledge of rock for a roof, but it kept him warm and protected his scientific instruments.

He drilled a straight line of holes all the way across the glacier and placed stakes with flags in the holes. By 1841 the flags were no longer in a straight line. All of them had moved forward with the ice.

That same summer Louis found a deep hole where melted snow had tunneled its way into the glacier. He ordered his assistants to lower him into the heart of the glacier. Sunlight filtering through the ice cast an eerie blue glow about him. Peering closely he saw beautiful blue-white layers caused by each winters's snowfall. It reminded him of growth rings of a tree.

The next year, Louis Agassiz spoke to the scientists again. This time he had proof. "We traced the movement of 18 boulders on a glacier," Louis said. "We made precise measurements and have proof that glaciers do move. We drove stakes into the ice and they moved, too. The stakes in the center moved faster than those at the edge."

He said, "When the Ice Age came, tropical vegetation of Europe was buried under a vast mantle of ice. All over, creation fell silent."

"Upon the life and movement of a powerful creation fell the silence of death. Springs paused, rivers ceased to flow, and the rays of the sun rising upon the frozen shore were met only by the breath of winter from the north and thunders of the crevasses as they opened across the surface of this icy sea."

Louis Agasiz won over his critics. A great Ice Age had struck the earth long ago.

In London, Paris, and Geneva scientific groups asked him to speak before them.

In 1846 scientists invited him to the United States. There he found many more signs of the Ice Age. Louis Agassiz concluded that ice had cut out the Mohawk

Beautiful Lake Geneva, Switzerland.

The maximum extent of the Ice Age in North America.

Valley and threw up Bunker Hill, site of the Revolutionary War battle.

When the North American Glacier melted, the water formed huge lakes. There are five Great Lakes, but at one time a sixth one filled the area in Northeast Minnesota, North Dakota, and the Canadian province of Manitoba.

Louis Agassiz mapped out its ancient shores. The lake was 700 miles long and almost 300 miles wide. It disappeared in time because most of it gradually drained into the Hudson Bay when the glaciers melted. It did, however, leave behind many small lakes.

Louis Agassiz decided to make the United States his home. "This is a land where nature was rich," he said.

He earned his living in America by teaching, something that came naturally to him. He could talk natural history with a professor or a stable boy. So popular did his lectures become that people bought tickets to hear him speak.

When he was out in the field, he would set up a black canvas cloth and use a piece of chalk to tell others about what he had learned. He told his students, "Study nature, not books. The best way to learn about the world of nature is to get outside and look at it carefully."

To this day Louis Agassiz is considered the greatest teacher of science who ever lived.

Shortly before the beginning of the American Civil War, Charles Darwin published a book, *Origin of Species*, in which he proposed the idea of evolution; that is, complex living organisms grew from nonliving matter. Could animals grow more complex through some unplanned happening? Darwin claimed that plants and animals died, only to be replaced by stronger, better ones.

Because Louis Agassiz was the best informed biologist of his day, many people wanted to know what he thought about evolution. Louis opposed the notion. He saw nature as part of the Creator's all-wise plan.

"The resources of the Deity," he said, "cannot be so meager that in order to create a human being He must change a monkey into a man."

Agassiz was a world explorer. He retraced the exact voyage Darwin made. "I made the voyage to study the whole Darwinian theory free from all external influence and former prejudices."

Louis sailed around the tip of South America and into the Pacific Ocean toward the Galapagos Islands. The Galapagos are about 600 miles off the coast of Ecuador.

Years before, Darwin had studied animals on the islands, which were home to many unusual creatures. Great tortoises and giant red lizards, called iguanas, lived on the Galapagos.

The sailors also caught a shark. Louis inspected it and said to his students, "Sharks have the largest brains, the most specialized teeth and muscular system. Judging from the nervous system alone, therefore, they should

Skier and friend enjoying the view of the Alps on a beautiful, clear day.

Charles Darwin sailed from Cambridge, England, in 1831, as a naturalist on board the HMS Beagle. He was a fan of Sir Charles Lyell, who did not believe the surface features of the earth were caused by Noah's flood, but by natural forces over long periods of time. Darwin soon began fitting his observations about nature into Lyell's theories (unproven beliefs).

When the Beagle arrived at the Galápagos Islands, off the coast of Ecuador, he began to apply his new theory to the things he observed. He noticed each island had its own variation of wildlife. He was also amazed by swimming iguanas (left).

On the islands Darwin noted 14 different species of finch. They had differently shaped bills to eat the food that was available. These varied from a tiny bill for eating insects to a large heavy bill for cracking hard seeds and nuts. Darwin concluded the different finches had evolved from a single finch that had landed on the islands in the past.

The Bible tells us in Genesis 1:11, 12, 21, 24, and 25 that God created the plants and animals "according to its kind." The finches that Darwin found on the Galápagos were still finches even though different shaped bills had developed. What Darwin had observed was natural selection.

"Natural selection is merely the interaction between organism and environment that weeds out harmful traits and allows helpful traits to become established. . . . Natural selection does not produce new characteristics. It only acts upon traits that already exist."[1] The theory of evolution says that one species can transform into another, such as a butterfly into a beetle. This is impossible without new genetic information.

Dogs could be used as an example of variations within a kind. There are more than a hundred different breeds of dogs (German Shepherd, poodle, rottweiler, etc.), but for all their differences — they are still dogs.

be regarded as the highest of fishes." Yet, according to the scheme of evolution they are very ancient fish.

When Louis returned to the United States, he went on record in opposition to the theory of evolution. He was the first person to do so for scientific reasons.

When Louis Agassiz died in 1873, his tombstone was made from a boulder found on the Aar Glacier. Honors came to his name even after his death. In 1915 he was elected to the Hall of Fame for Great Americans. The ghost lake, the sixth Great Lake near Lake Superior, was named Lake Agassiz in his honor.

Louis Agassiz looked upon his success as only seeing the order put in the universe by the Creator. He found in nature a constant reminder of God. "God writes the books of nature," Louis said. "I am only His librarian."

[1] Davis, Percival and Dean H. Kenyon, Of Pandas and People (Dallas, TX, Haughton Publishing Company), p. 10.

Questions

Into the Heart of the Glacier

Choose A or B to complete the sentence.

1. Ice covers the Antarctic and
    A. Australia.
    B. Greenland.

2. Professor Cuvier believed fossils were caused by
    A. a series of worldwide disasters.
    B. slow changes in the earth's climate.

3. Louis Agassiz showed that glaciers
    A. are locked into position.
    B. move like slow rivers.

4. The Great Lakes were formed by
    A. melting glaciers.
    B. underground springs.

5. Louis Agassiz believed the best way to learn about nature was to
    A. get outside and look at it carefully.
    B. study books.

CHAPTER 14

RIVERS— EARTH'S LIFELINE

Rivers are the lifeline of earth. Most great countries and important cities grew up on the banks of rivers. Even the Garden of Eden was watered by a river that divided into four rivers: Pishon, Havilah, Tigris, and Euphrates.

The longest rivers on earth are the Nile of Africa, the Amazon of South America, the Mississippi-Missouri of North America, and the Yangtze of Asia. Each of these rivers is more than 3,700 miles long.

Herodotus, who lived 2,000 ago, called Egypt "the gift of the Nile." Egypt grew up in the heart

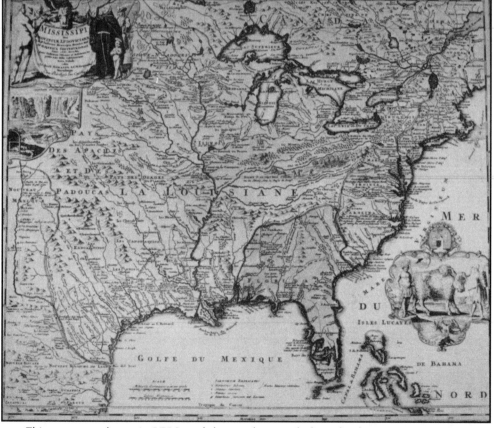

This map was drawn in 1719 and shows what was believed to be an accurate depiction of the area the Mississippi River covered.

High on a cliff at Abu Simbel sits the Great Temple. The temple was built about 1270 B.C. by Pharaoh Ramses II in his own honor. Each of the statues of Ramses is 67 feet high and weighs 1,200 tons. The Small Temple, dedicated to his queen, Nefertari, is just to the right (not seen in photo).

When the Aswan High Dam was built a reservoir named Lake Nasser began to form. The valleys behind the dam would soon be underwater. Since the *temples had originally been built in one of these valleys an international organization was formed to save them. An army of skilled workers began a rescue operation. When lake rose faster than they expected an 80-foot high earthen dam was built in front of the temples to protect the work. The temples were cut into blocks, numbered, raised, and reassembled 212 feet higher and 67 feet back. If they had not been raised you would need scuba gear to visit them.*

of deserts to become the first great empire. All along the banks of the Nile are monuments, expensive tombs, temples, the pyramids, and the Sphinx that show the glories of ancient Egypt.

Egypt is a dry land. Egyptians don't talk about the weather. Instead, they talk about the Nile; whether it is clear or muddy, shallow, or about to flood.

Even today the waters of the Nile turn the bordering desert into the most fertile farmland on earth. Crops in the rich black soil grow two and a half times better than on farmland elsewhere.

Along the Nile's banks grows papyrus, the reedlike plant from which paper was first made. Along the same banks, Miriam watched over the floating crib of her baby brother Moses, who was being hidden from Pharaoh (read Exod. 2:3-8).

Egyptian clay vases made thousands of years ago have drawings on them of the earliest known sailing craft. The Nile is a friendly river for sailing ships. Ships float

Most school children on a field trip visit museums or parks. The school children of Cairo, in the bottom photo, are visiting a great pyramid. Some people think of the pyramids as being out in the desert, but there are high-rise office buildings only six miles from where these children are sitting.

downriver to the Mediterranean sea. There the cargo is unloaded, and tall sails are raised. The sails reach high above the surface of the river to catch faint desert breezes. Because of prevailing winds, ships can sail back up-stream.

Ships go upriver with the wind, and downriver with the current. It's a free trip both ways!

The Nile is an unusual river, for it flows from south to north almost in a straight line. It reaches a tenth of the way around the world. For most of its 4,000 miles the Nile runs straight through deserts.

Summer after summer it brings life-giving moisture to scorching deserts where rain never falls. Since it does run through deserts, what is the source of its water? How can the Nile keep on flowing even during the hottest and driest summers?

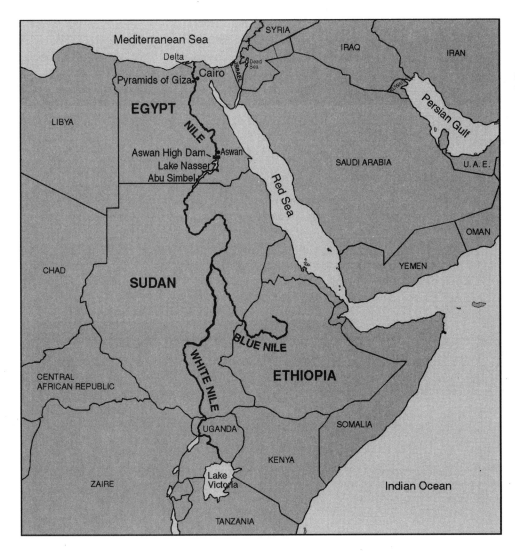

The great Nile has been called a "gigantic serpent." It is fed by many other smaller rivers, but its two main sources are the 2,285-mile White Nile and the 1,080-mile Blue Nile. After they join together they flow northward to the delta and empty into the Mediterranean Sea.

The Nile begins as melting snow in the mountains of Africa's great central highlands. Snow is a form of water storage. The heavy snows on the slopes of high mountains remain there until summer. Then they melt providing water all summer long. In this way, land along the Nile can support crops all summer.

The Bible mentions "treasures of snow" in the Book of Job (Job 38:22). Perhaps this refers to the fact that snow stores water.

The Nile is a super river in length, but not in the amount of water it carries. Most of the water from the melting snow evaporates as it passes through dry deserts.

The Amazon, on the other hand, carries 20 times as much water as the Nile. The Amazon is the biggest river by far. All of the rivers in the United States combined — including the Mississippi — carry less water than the Amazon does. Of every 100 gallons of water that drain into the sea, 20 gallons come from the Amazon. That's more than the six next largest rivers combined.

The Amazon's huge size is difficult to imagine. More than 500 other rivers flow into it. It drains more than one-half of South America. It comes within 60 miles of cutting South America in half and connecting the Atlantic to the Pacific.

The Amazon is almost exactly 4,000 miles in length. That makes it the second-longest river in the world. For much of its length the Amazon is five miles wide. Near its mouth, where it flows into the ocean, it is too wide to see across. Ships 200 miles out in the Atlantic sail through the muddy red stains of water carried to the ocean by the Amazon.

In 1541 two Spanish adventurers, Gonzalo Pizarro and Francisco Orellana (pictured at left) met in Peru and set out with 200 men in search of El Dorado (a fabled land of gold) believed to be in the Andes Mountains. They ran out of food and ended up eating their leather belts and shoe soles "cooked with certain herbs." Pizarro sent Orellana and 57 men in search of food. They took boats and traveled down the Napo River (in what is now Ecuador). They finally found food 700 miles downriver. They believed they could not get back upstream and continued downriver. They reached the mouth of the Amazon on August 26, 1542. When he returned to Spain King Charles I appointed Orellana as governor of the land he had explored. When he returned to the Amazon he caught a fever and died in 1546 at the age of 35.

The Amazon River is the largest watershed (area drained by a river) in the world. It drains an area of more than 2.3 million square miles. Yearly it accounts for one-fifth of all fresh water that drains into the oceans of the world. So much fresh water flows into the Atlantic Ocean that 100 miles from shore it is still more like freshwater than saltwater.

Francisco de Orellana (OH-ray-YAW-nah), a Spaniard, was the first European to explore the Amazon River. Orellana and his party started from Peru and followed the Napo River to the Amazon. His party drifted down the river, reaching the Atlantic in August 1542.

Along the way, a group of female warriors attacked his party, or so he claimed. In any event, he gave the river its name. In Greek mythology, the Amazons were a race of women warriors who fought with the Trojans against the Greeks in the Trojan Wars. Francisco de Orellana named the river after the women warriors.

Heavy rainfall makes the land along the Amazon a jungle with dense undergrowth

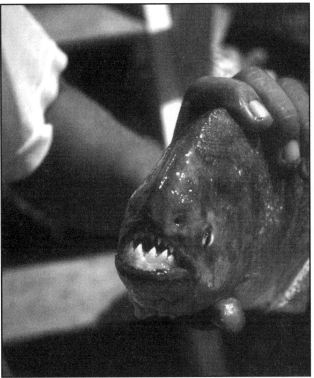

The Amazon is a strange and wonderful place. But for those who have not learned how to survive, it can also be deadly. The river itself can be full of creatures you wouldn't meet up with by choice. The piranha above is a good example. There are also electric eels and a variety of water-loving snakes to be cautious about.

The man in the canoe is dwarfed by the wall of jungle behind him. It is so dense that you can often go for miles along the banks of the Amazon and its tributaries and not find a place to go onto land.

and thick forest. It is the world's largest rain forest. Deep in the forest grow ironwood, mahogany, rubber trees (from which South American natives made the first rubber balls), and balsa (the lightest of all woods). This valuable lumber is difficult to transport overland. The rain forest has only a few trails and even fewer roads.

The river is the one reliable means of transportation. The Amazon is perfect for river traffic. Its course is very gentle. Two-thirds of the river system is navigable, and there are no falls or rapids. The Amazon and its tributaries are South America's best "highways." They have carried the canoes of Indians, the ships of determined missionaries, and the rafts of early settlers.

Another of the earth's great rivers is the Yangtze, in central China. It is the longest river in Asia and the fourth-longest river in the world. Rising in northeastern Tibet, the river flows 3,716 miles to the East China Sea.

A Chinese farmer plows his fields with the help of a water buffalo just as his ancestors had done for hundreds of generations.

Of all the people on earth, one out of every eight lives along the banks of the Yangtze. Six of China's largest cities, each with a population of more than a million people, are on the Yangtze system.

Ancient books call the Yangtze the "great river." In China it is called the Ch'ang Chiang, which merely means "the long river."

The Yangtze's source is in Tibet, the summit of the great Himalaya mountain range. Mt. Everest, the highest mountain on earth, is found in Tibet. The Yangtze begins below the wildest and most beautiful snow-capped mountains in the world.

In Asia, where there are few highways and railroads, the life and commerce of China depends upon rivers. For centuries the Yangtze has been a great way to travel. Marco Polo used it on his travels. He calculated that in a five-year period a million boats passed by one city where he lived.

Unlike the Amazon, the Yangtze is a dangerous river — it is the most difficult river in the world to navigate. The rushing current cuts through a series of awe-inspiring gorges. It narrows to only 50 yards across, zigzagging between rocky cliffs that rise a half mile on either side.

In places the current is so swift that boats have to be pulled by donkeys on paths cut in the rocky cliffs. At one time as many as 1 in every 20 ships were wrecked as they made their way through the wild and dangerous gorges.

But after shooting through the canyon walls, the Yangtze becomes a pleasant river important for irrigation of rice fields. Like a main street, the river is a maze of traffic. There are river boats with brightly colored sails, creaking junks, family sampans, steamers, and tugs.

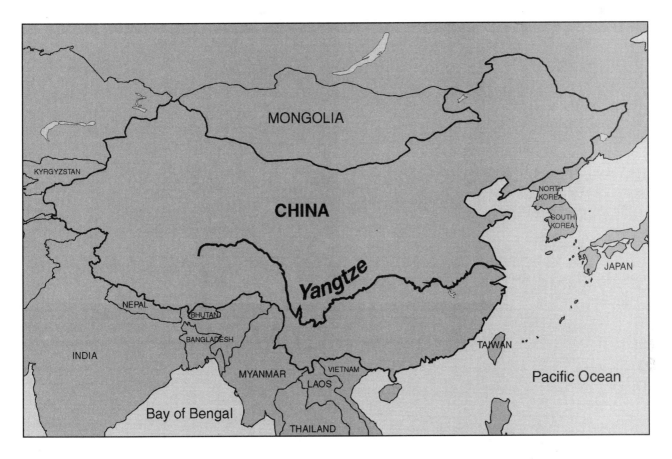

The Yangtze is the longest river in Asia and the fourth longest in the world. The Chinese know the river as Ch'ang Chiang (long river) or simply as Chiang (the river). One of the narrow gorges it runs through is called Tiger Leap Gorge. Legend tells of a tiger leaping from one bank to the other.

But the importance of a river isn't judged by length alone. The Thames, the Seine, and the Hudson Rivers are short, but they serve the important cities of London, Paris, and New York.

Look at the Jordan River in Palestine. This small river, only 200 miles long, begins in the foothills of Mount Hermon, flows though the lakes of Huleh and Galilee, and on into the Dead Sea. More than half of the Jordan's length is below sea level.

Yet this tiny, unimportant-looking, muddy river is filled with history. Here, Joshua led the children of the slaves of Egypt into the land promised them by God. In the muddy waters Naaman washed clean his leprosy. John the Baptist preached on its shores. Jesus was baptized there.

Rivers don't circulate water only — they circulate life as well. A river, regardless of its length or size, is an important part of the earth's water system. Countries like the United States need about a million gallons of water per person every year. This water is used for drinking, washing, on farms, and in factories. The water must be free of harmful germs and dangerous chemicals.

Rivers keep flowing, always flowing. Far upstream clean rain water and water from melting snows tumbles along in cool brooks. The water falls over rocks and splashes into the air. This constant motion of water helps purify it. On the average, a river empties the land through which it flows once every two weeks. Rivers start fresh water circulating across the land.

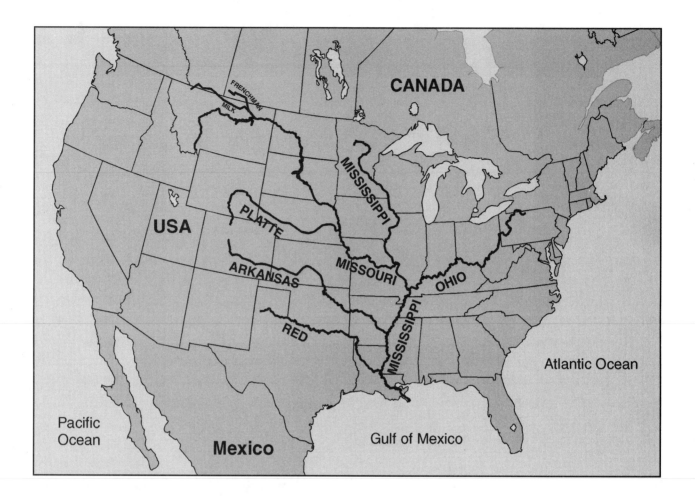

weeks. Rivers start fresh water circulating across the land.

The Bible describes the water cycle like this: "All the rivers run into the sea; yet the sea is not full; unto the place from whence the rivers come, thither they return again" (Eccles. 1:7).

The mighty Mississippi River, like all large rivers, is fed by other smaller rivers. The waterfall on the left is typical of thousands of small rivers that rush to meet up with larger ones. Each one adds to the volume of the next. The Missouri River is longer, but the Mississippi River carries a greater volume of water.

Rivers — Earth's Lifeline

Identify each description as being of the Nile, Amazon, or Yangtze.

1. Along its banks are pyramids _____

2. Flows through central Asia _____

3. Flows through desert _____

4. Flows through rain forest _____

5. Has a swift current through deep gorges _____

6. Has more than 500 tributaries _____

7. Its source is in Tibet _____

8. Largest river (by water flow) _____

9. Longest river _____

10. Moses was hidden in a floating crib upon this river _____

11. Named after a fearsome tribe of female warriors _____

12. Papyrus grows along its banks _____

Thought Question:

13. What is a great river in your area? Why do you consider it great?

_____

_____

CHAPTER 15

THE MYSTERIOUS VALLEY

In 1541, Hernando de Soto, a Spanish explorer, discovered the Mississippi. Of course, native Americans knew about the river all along. The Indians who lived on the river called it Mississippi, which in their language meant "big river."

The source of the Mississippi was found to be from Lake Itasca in Minnesota. There the mighty river is only a trickle ten feet across and less than a foot deep.

In 1803, the United States bought the Louisiana Territory from France. Napoleon needed the money to pursue his wars with England. The French sold all the land that was drained by the western tributaries that flowed into the Mississippi.

Norris Basin in Yellowstone National Park is even magnificent in the winter because of the billowing steam produced in the cold air.

As the clear lake water from the Upper Mississippi flows along near St. Louis, Missouri, brown muddy water joins it from the Missouri River which comes from the west. The waters flow side by side for miles before the brown water of the Missouri mingles with the clear water from the north.

The exact extent of the Louisiana territory wasn't known. No one had completely explored the Missouri River. In 1804 Meriwether Lewis and William Clark set out to explore the new territory. They left St. Louis in 1804 and backtracked the Missouri River to its source in the Rocky Mountains — a total distance 2,500 miles.

Today, mapmakers and scientists consider the Missouri-Mississippi the main river. The Upper Mississippi is a tributary. This makes the Missouri-Mississippi the longest river in North America. It is 3,800 miles long — the third-longest river in the world.

At one time the Missouri-Mississippi was the longest river in the world, even longer than the Nile. But it is shorter now.

It seems strange to think that a river can change in length, but each year a river gets longer by meandering in new directions, or gets shorter by taking short cuts through new channels. During a single year the Mississippi may change its path by 50 miles.

During the Lewis and Clark expedition, they heard rumors of a hidden valley at the headwaters of the Yellowstone River high in the mountains of Wyoming. According to the rumor, springs in this mysterious valley shot hot water into the air. The land simmered with bubbling mud. Clouds of steam rose from the rivers that bubbled out of the ground.

Yellowstone Falls, Yellowstone National Park

Most people laughed at these stories. They said a few old mountain men made up these fantastic stories. John Colter, a mountain man, first described the Yellowstone country in 1808. In the next 50 years, only four other people claimed to have reached the valley and gotten out safely. In 1859 a party sponsored by the United States government set out for Yellowstone, but they failed to reach the fabled valley.

William Henry Jackson liked to explore the wide, wild country of the American West. That's why he hired out as a photographer for a railway company. As they laid

Lewis and Clark

Meriwether Lewis

William Clark

The Pacific at last! They reached the mouth of the Columbia River on September 23, 1806. They accomplished what no one had done before. When they returned they received a hero's welcome. In 1807 Lewis became the governor of the Louisiana Territory. Clark became a superintendent of Indian affairs. He adopted Sacagawea's son Jean Baptiste, who was born on the trail. He sent the boy to Europe to be educated and Jean later worked as a guide for travelers heading west.

In North Dakota Lewis and Clark hired a French-Canadian trapper to serve as interpreter. His wife Sacagawea (SAK-uh-jah-WEE-uh), a Shoshone Indian, came too. She proved to be more useful than her husband because her presence made it easier to make friends with the Indians they met on their trip.

track and cut tunnels, William Henry Jackson took pictures.

At that time photography was something new. Most photographers were happy to stay at home and take portraits inside well-lighted studios. Not William Henry Jackson. He was one of the first to photograph the waterfalls, deep mountain canyons, and snow-covered mountain peaks of the Rocky Mountains. But he wanted to photograph the even stranger sights of the American West where the railway hadn't been built.

William Henry Jackson's pictures for the railroads came to the attention of Ferdinand Hayden, an explorer for the United States government. Hayden planned to lead an expedition into the Rocky Mountains.

Hayden wanted to thoroughly exlore the Yellowstone valley. He usually took an official artist to draw the sights along the route. This time he decided to take a photographer, too. He offered the position to William Henry Jackson. All of Jackson's equipment would have to fit on one mule. That in itself was a difficult task, because Jackson needed 500 plate glass negatives, two huge cameras, several boxes of chemicals, and a special darkroom tent. But he succeeded in packing everything upon a burro named Maud.

The northwest corner of Wyoming was surrounded on all sides by tall mountains. Once, the expedition made a difficult climb up the steep side of a cliff. Maud lost her footing on the treacherous trail. The burro fell 30 feet. The animal landed upside-down in a scrubby tree. The burro struggled free, completely unhurt. She rejoined the end of the line as if nothing had happened.

The Hayden expedition arrived in the Yellowstone region in the summer of 1871. They camped by a mammoth hot spring

which had formed a dome-shaped hill. The hill had terraces like giant steps.

They found pools of colorful mud that bubbled like a large pudding. The

Multnomah Falls is in the Columbia River Gorge. Lewis and Clark probably saw it as they floated by it on the Columbia River.

Yellowstone River had cut a deep gorge. The river fell in two stupendous falls. Its walls were of red, pink, yellow, white, and a hundred rainbow colors. The Yellowstone River combined Niagara Falls, the Painted Desert, and the Grand Canyon into one fantastic spectacle.

The explorers came across a petrified forest and a mountain of black glass. The glass, obsidian, is a natural black glass found near volcanos.

All the rumors about the wonderful valley were true after all.

Jackson took photographs of all of this. At every new sight he set up his special darkroom tent. He unpacked the camera. Quickly he mixed chemicals, coated the glass negative, snapped the picture, and rushed back to the tent to develop the picture.

William Henry Jackson left the expedition to explore further. He discovered a geyser that shot hot water almost 200 feet into the air. The eruptions came every hour without fail. He called the geyser Old Faithful. He discovered Old Faithful and was the first to photograph it. It is still the most photographed sight in Yellowtone.

When Hayden's expedition left the mysterious valley, they were convinced they had made a real discovery. Nowhere else in the world were there so many awesome spectacles.

"This land should be saved for all to see," Jackson said.

Old Faithful is the most photographed spot in Yellowstone National Park.

Hayden explained, "The government gives land to anyone who will settle it. Soon Yellowstone will become the property of a hundred different homesteaders."

Hayden's expedition returned to Washington, DC, and urged Congress to set aside the valley as a park. The senators hesitated. This was an unusual idea.

Some senators didn't believe the reports. Thomas Moran, a famous artist, had made drawings of Yellowstone — but he might have exaggerated what he saw.

Then William Henry Jackson stepped forward with his photographs. He put them on display at the Capitol.

The photographs worked. Yellowstone became the nations's —and the world's — first national park.

William Henry Jackson's display showed the importance of photography to scientific exploration. From then on, photography became an important tool of scientists as they explored the earth.

Questions

The Mysterious Valley

Choose A or B to complete the sentence.

1. The first European to see the Mississippi River was

   A. Hernando de Soto.

   B. Napoleon.

2. The Louisiana Territory was made of all

   A. land drained by rivers that flow into the Mississippi from the west.

   B. states that border Louisiana.

3. Lewis and Clark traced the Missouri river back to its source in the

   A. Arctic tundra.

   B. Rocky Mountains.

4. The Missouri-Mississippi is

   A. surprisingly short.

   B. the third longest river in the world.

5. Old Faithful was first photographed by

   A. William Henry Jackson.

   B. a mountain man.

Thought Questions:

6. Explain the role of photography in helping make Yellowstone the world's first national park.

   _____

   _____

7. List five natural sights found in Yellowstone

   _____

   _____

CHAPTER 16

THE ATMOSPHERE

Of the three spheres of earth — lithosphere (rock), hydrosphere (water), and atmosphere (air) — the atmosphere was the last one to be explored in detail. Until the time of Galileo in the early 1600s, people ignored the atmosphere. They didn't think of air as an actual existence like rock or water. Instead, they thought of air as some sort of mysterious "spirit."

The first person to investigate the atmosphere was Evangelista Torricelli (tor-rih-CHEL-lee). He served as Galileo's assistant during the last three years of Galileo's life. Evangelista was asked to explain why the best water pumps couldn't lift water higher than 34 feet. He came to the

19th century aneroid barometer

conclusion that air does have weight. It is a physical substance, just like rock, or water. Of course, a cubic foot of air weighs far less than a cubic foot of rock or water. A cubic foot of rock weighs about 200 pounds. A cubic foot of water weighs about 65 pounds. A cubic foot of air weighs about one and a half ounces.

The kind of water pump Evangelista studied raised water by pumping air from a pipe. The pressure of the outside air forced water up into the pipe. When the weight of the water raised in the pipe equaled the weight of the air, the water could rise no farther.

This allowed Evangelista to compare the weight of the air to the weight of water. Imagine two pipes. Both pipes are one foot across. One pipe is 34 feet high. It is filled with water. The other pipe extends from the surface of the earth to the top of the atmosphere. It is filled with air, Although the sample of water is far smaller than the sample of air, both weigh the same.

The atmosphere does have weight, and the weight is considerable. Each square inch of the earth's surface — or your own body — has a weight of 14.7 pounds pressing upon it. The weight due to air is known as air pressure. Usually we don't feel this pressure. The air within your body is equal to the outside pressure, so they cancel one another. But when you change elevation rapidly, your ears "pop" due to the changing air pressure.

Torricelli realized that experiments with air pressure could be more easily conducted by using mercury rather than water. Mercury, a liquid metal, is 13.6 times as heavy as

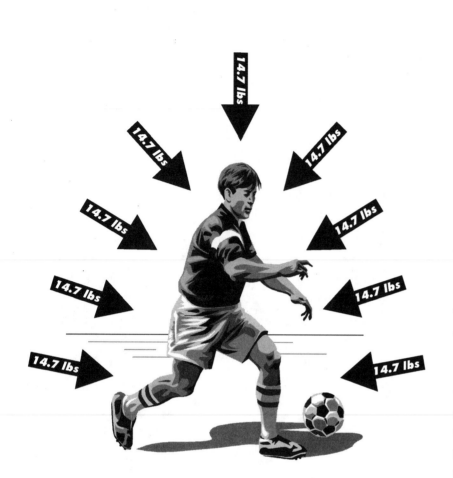

with his finger and up-ended the tube in a dish of mercury. When he removed his finger the mercury partially drained from the tube. But a column of mercury 30 inches high was left in the tube.

Some scholars believed the mercury was supported by the vacuum above the mercury, They claimed that "nature abhors a vacuum." But Torricelli concluded that the liquid was supported by the outside air pressing on the mercury in the open dish.

Mercury drains from the tube until the pressure of its own weight inside the tube equals the outside atmospheric pressure upon the mercury in the dish.

The height of the mercury is usually about 30 inches. Its height does change from day to day due to slight changes in the air pressure. Torricelli had invented the first *barometer*, a device that measures air pressure.

Atmospheric pressure becomes less with height above sea level. In 1648, Blaise Pascal (pas-KAL), a French scientist, wondered how the height of a mercury column in a barometer would change if carried up a mountain. Pascal himself was in delicate health. He designed the experiment, but he looked for someone else to carry it out.

Pascal gave his brother-in-law a barometer and sent him up the side of a mountain. The brother-in-law measured air pressure at a height of one mile. He found that the mercury column had fallen by about one-tenth of its original height. This meant that about one-tenth of the atmosphere is found below one mile.

As the soccer player pivots to kick the ball he is surrounded by 14.7 pound of air pressure every way he turns. If he were playing in Mexico City (7,710 ft.) or Denver, Colorado (called the mile high city because it is at 5, 280 ft.), he would be playing in less air pressure than if he were playing at sea level.

the same volume of water. For that reason, a column of mercury would need to be only 1/13.6 times as high as a column of water — about 30 inches instead of 34 feet.

Torricelli filled with mercury a long glass tube closed at one end and open at the other. He capped the open end of the tube

How high is the atmosphere? Most of the atmosphere is found near the earth's surface. As mountain climbers gain altitude they notice that the air becomes thinner. A mountain climber at an altitude of 18,500 feet (about 3.5 miles) finds the pressure to be only 15 inches of mercury, only half the sea level value of 30 inches of mercury.

Three-fourths of the atmosphere is found below 35,000 feet. The tops of some thunderclouds reach this height. But the atmosphere doesn't stop there. The glowing trails of shooting stars (meteorites) are due to air friction. Meteorites begin glowing at about 100 miles, showing that the atmosphere extends that far. The glow of the northern lights, aurora borealis, is even higher.

The atmosphere has no definite boundary. It simply fades off gradually into the near emptiness of space. Even

Blaise Pascal was a French philosopher, mathematician and physicist. By age 16 he had shown himself to be a mathematical genius and at 19 invented the first mechanical adding machine.

Pascal was a deeply religious man who believed in and trusted God. In his book, Pensees, he talks about the difference between trusting God and not trusting Him. Dr. Henry Morris, in his book Men of Science, Men of God, paraphrases Pascal's beliefs, "How can anyone lose who chooses to become a Christian?"

An Altimeter is used to measure height above sea level.

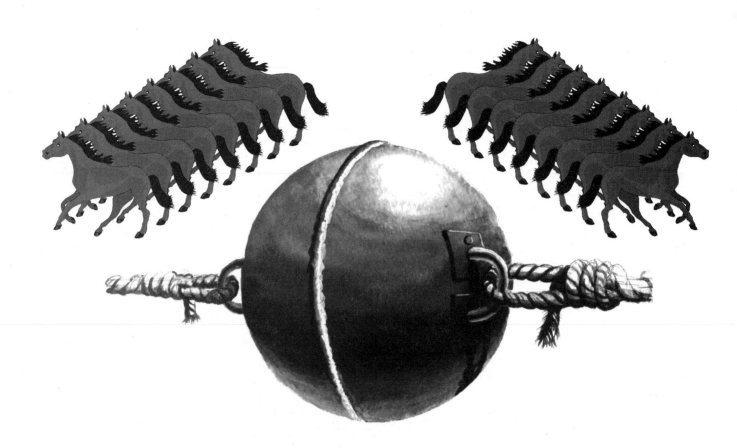

In what had to be one of the most spectacular science experiments of the day Guericke demonstrated the importance of air pressure. In the process he invented the first air pump.

out as far as 300 miles, a thin wisp of air molecules can be detected.

A barometer can be used to measure elevation. When used in this way, a barometer is called an altimeter. The word *altimeter* means "altitude meter." It is used by pilots of balloons and airplanes to measure their height above sea level.

One of the most dramatic experiments showing the powerful pressure of the air was conducted in 1654. Otto von Guericke (GAY-rih-kuh), the city magistrate of Magdeburg, Germany, was an amateur scientist. He read about the discoveries of Torricelli and Pascal. He grew so interested in the subject of air pressure that he designed and built the first air pump. With it he could partially pump the air out of a container.

He made two copper bowls, each about two feet across. Each bowl was a hemisphere, a half of a sphere. He placed the two copper hemispheres together to form a sphere. He filled the seam around them with wax to make them airtight.

Otto von Guericke attached his air pump to one of the hemispheres and pumped out most of the air. Guericke hooked an eight-horse team to each hemisphere. He had them pulling in opposite directions, trying to separate the hemispheres. The hemispheres couldn't be pulled apart.

Then Otto von Guericke opened the valve and let air inside the hemispheres. By letting air into the globe, the outside and inside air pressures were equalized. The two hemispheres fell apart.

The next person to study the mystery of the atmosphere was Robert Boyle. He was the seventh son in a family of 14 children. His father was Richard Boyle, the Great Earl of Cork, one of the most respected and wealthy men in Ireland. The Great Earl of Cork was a thrifty, hard working, and religious man.

Robert Boyle's father wanted his children to appreciate God's blessings and learn the importance of hard work. He especially didn't want his children to be spoiled and idle. Each year for several weeks he sent his children on a "vacation." The children lived with a peasant family. They slept, ate, and worked with the poor family.

As a child, Robert Boyle traveled widely as part of his education. He visited Italy in 1641, spent the winter in Florence, and met Galileo shortly before that great scientist's death. Not all of his travels were pleasant excursions. Once, at age 11, he was caught in the Swiss Alps when a terrifying thunderstorm struck. Later, Robert said, "It seemed like the end of the world."

Early in life, he developed the habit of praying and reading from the Bible each morning. In later life, Boyle often stated that the hand of God had protected him during his travels. He became England's best known scientist in the time right before Isaac

Late spring in the Swiss Alps is beautiful and the air is crisp and clean.

Robert Boyle is one of the founders of the Royal Society of London and considered to be the father of modern chemistry. He was also a humble, witnessing Christian who spent much of his time studying the Bible. Boyle was dedicated to mission work and spent much of his own money for Bible translation work.

knowledge in all fields, including the Bible. He learned Hebrew and Greek in order to better understand the word of God.

He believed that the future of scientific discovery lay in the use of experiments. Most scientists of his time didn't perform experiments to learn new information. Instead, they looked up the correct "answers" in books by ancient Greeks.

Robert Boyle's motto, "nothing by mere authority," rejected the current belief that all answers in science could be found in the old books.

In 1654, Robert Boyle moved to Oxford, the scientific center of England. He began weekly meetings with several people who would later become very famous indeed. Christopher Wren would rebuild London after the great fire of 1666. Isaac Barlow would "discover" Isaac Newton. Robert Hooke would help Boyle carry out a series of important experiments. It was an exciting time. The group held informal talks in each other's homes and in coffee shops. Robert Boyle called the group the "invisible college" because of the many new ideas they discussed.

One member of the "invisible college" described Otto von Guericke's experiments with the air pump. In 1657, Robert Boyle designed an improved air pump. His assistant, Robert Hooke, built it. They perfected Guericke's crude design. Fifty years passed

Newton. As the years passed and his fame spread, he became even more dedicated to the service of God.

Robert Boyle became one of the first modern scientists. The word *science* is from a Latin word meaning "knowledge." Robert Boyle believed a true scientist must have before anyone improved upon Boyle's design or surpassed his skill at using it.

Robert Boyle's air pump made possible an unusual experiment. He placed a feather and lump of lead inside a glass cylinder and pumped out the air. When he turned the cylinder upside down, both feather and lead fell side by side. This proved what Galileo had guessed: all bodies fall at the same speed in a vacuum. A feather only falls slower than a piece of lead because of air resistance. Take away the air and they both fall at the same speed.

The air pump became as important as a microscope and telescope to scientists. It opened many new fields for them to explore: the speed of sound, weather, air pressure, combustion (burning), and respiration (breathing).

Only in a vacuum can a feather and piece of lead fall at the same rate.

One of Boyle's experiments hinted at the connection between combustion and respiration. He showed that charcoal would not burn in a closed vessel with the air pumped out.

In another experiment he placed a bird in a glass jar and began pumping out the air. But when he saw the bird was dying, his tender nature overcame his scientific curiosity. He stopped the experiment and rescued the bird. "I released it to freedom to repay its suffering," he said.

The study did show that living things do need air to breath. Everybody knows this fact today, but they didn't until after Boyle's experiment.

Doctors compared Boyle's pump with the heart and saw that they were remarkably alike. For the first time, the true nature of circulation of blood became easier to understand.

The pump was a commercial success, too. It could pump water as well as air. Miners used it to pump out flooded mines. Sailors used it to bail water.

Boyle's studies replaced idle thoughts with a solid foundation of careful experiments. Boyle believed strongly that all experiment work should be quickly reported so others might learn of new discoveries.

How could useful ideas be spread more easily? Robert Boyle remembered the "invisible college." Scientists gained a lot by meeting together often. Robert Boyle brought the matter before Charles II. The king chartered the group of scholars as the Royal Society. It still meets today.

In science, one of his greatest achievements was to open the atmosphere to exploration. Columbus discovered the new world. Robert Boyle discovered the atmosphere.

Stone and water cannot be compressed. Air is another matter. Robert Boyle showed that air can be compressed. In his scientific paper, "The Spring of the Air," he described one of his most important discoveries. Robert Boyle found a simple law that described how the air's volume changed. By doubling the pressure, the air was squeezed into half the space. By making the pressure four times as great, the air was squeezed into one-fourth its original space.

This discovery of how pressure changes the volume of air is known as Boyle's Law.

Robert Boyle's studies also marked the first steps toward meteorology, the study of weather. He noticed that the mercury level in a barometer fell shortly before a storm.

Atmospheric pressure can change from one day to the next due to changing weather conditions. A steady, high barometer predicts fair weather. A rapidly falling barometer means a storm is approaching. A low pressure is one in which the mercury column falls in the tube. A low pressure indicates foul weather.

In 1680, fellow scientists elected Robert Boyle president of the Royal Society. He turned down the office to devote more time to spreading the gospel. Throughout his life, Robert Boyle read the Bible each morning, in spite of illness, eye trouble, and the press of his other duties. He wrote many papers about religion and science. He provided funds for a new Irish translation of the entire Bible. He gave away thousands of the Bibles.

When Robert Boyle died on December 30, 1691, he left his estate to various Christian works. His will provided for a series of lectures, not on science, but upon the Christian religion. Today, Robert Boyle is remembered for his discoveries about the atmosphere, as a founder of the Royal Society, and for his Christian faith.

In science, one of his greatest achievements was to open the atmosphere to exploration. Columbus discovered the New World. Robert Boyle discovered the atmosphere.

Questions

The Atmosphere

Choose A or B to complete the sentence.

1. Evangelista Torricelli used mercury in a long glass tube to measure

    A. atmospheric pressure.

    B. depth of a water well.

2. A barometer

    A. is an air pump.

    B. measures air pressure.

3. An altimeter is a

    A. barometer that measures height above sea level.

    B. special type of water pump.

4. Blaise Pascal showed that as one climbs a mountain, air pressure becomes

    A. greater.

    B. less.

5. Otto von Guericke showed that air pressure could hold together two spheres

    A. except during a lightning storm.

    B. against the pull of two teams of horses.

6. Robert Boyle showed that air

    A. follows laws of science.

    B. is a mysterious substance that follows no set laws.

Thought Question:

7. What was the "invisible college"?

_____

_____

8. Although Robert Hooke built the improved air pump, Robert Boyle is given credit as the inventor of the improved pump. Why is this?

_____

_____

CHAPTER 17

EXPLORING BY BALLOON

Joseph and Jacques Montgolfier (mohn-gohl-FYAY) were two of the 16 children of a paper manufacturer. They lived in Annonay, France. One day, Joseph threw a paper bag into a fire. Hot air filled the paper bag and sent it flying up the chimney.

The two brothers made a bigger paper bag. They held it over a fire, letting it fill with hot air. When they released the bag, it soared into the air. Hot air was lighter than cold air. To the brothers' delight, they discovered that the bigger the bag, the heavier the load it could carry aloft. Larger bags stayed aloft longer and soared higher.

Many of the early balloons were works of art. The French have a flair for taking ordinary things and making them beautiful.

The father realized his sons had hit upon an important discovery. He agreed to pay for a public demonstration of a hot air balloon. On June 5, 1783, in the market square of Annonay, thousands of people from miles around assembled to watch the spectacle. The balloon was 35 feet in diameter and weighed 300 pounds.

At a signal, assistants cut the ropes holding the balloon down. With a shout from the crowd, the balloon floated slowly into the sky. It reached a height of a thousand feet. The balloon drifted along for ten minutes before coming to rest a mile and a half from the launch site.

It was an unmanned balloon. Later that year marked the first time people actually became airborne.

In November the Montgolfiers built a balloon to be flown in Paris. It was made of linen cloth lined with paper. They painted it a dazzling blue and gold and decorated its sides with bright designs. Even standing still the giant balloon was an imposing sight.

The Montgolfier balloon had a diameter of 54 feet and could hold 55,000 cubic feet of hot air. Each cubic foot of hot air lifted

Many of the greatest discoveries have been made because someone was paying attention and started to ask questions. People had watched birds fly since the beginning and wished they could be soaring too. Finally that long held dream was about to come true. The first steps toward reaching for the stars was unfolding in France in 1783. One-hundred and eighty-six years later, in 1969, a human being would be standing on the moon.

Hot air ballooning has become a worldwide sport. The balloons come in all shapes and sizes — not just the typical shape seen above. One of the largest balloon races in the world is held every year in Albuquerque, New Mexico.

about a half ounce, so the balloon could carry 1,700 pounds. They built a ring-shaped wicker basket at the bottom of the balloon to carry passengers.

At first King Louis XVI of France disapproved of sending people aloft. He feared the flight might be too risky. Then he suggested that criminals under sentence of death should fly the balloon.

Pilatre de Rozier, a young nobleman, was aghast at the thought. "Criminals shouldn't have the honor of being the first humans to rise in the sky," he said. Pilatre de Rozier and a friend, the Marquis d'Arlandes, volunteered to test the balloon.

King Louis relented. "Away to the heavens you go. May God go with you. I give you my royal blessing."

On November 21, 1783, an enormous crowd of spectators came to see Pilatre and the Marquis off. Present was King Louis XVI, Marie Antoinette, and the entire royal family. Also watching in the crowds was the

United States representative to France — Benjamin Franklin.

Three hundred thousand people gasped in amazement as the balloon rose into the air. De Rozier and the Marquis threw piles of straw upon the fire and kept it blazing. They rose to 500 feet. The crowded cheered.

Then, suddenly, disaster threatened. Sparks from the fire began burning holes in the balloon. But the two pilots had come prepared. They dipped sponges in buckets of water. By holding the sponges on long poles, they succeeded in putting out the patches of fire.

The two brave sky travelers landed five miles from their starting point. Pilatre de Rozier and the Marquis d'Arlandes became the first human beings to fly a lighter-than-air craft.

Scientists of the French Academy of Science observed the flight. They found it incredible that the Montgolfier brothers carried out what others only dreamed about. Why? The two brothers were amateurs and not scientists at all.

Professor Jacques Charles (pro-nounced in the French manner as "Zhock Shahrl") studied the Montgolfier balloons. The lift came from hot air which floats in cold air, just like wood floats on water.

"Hot air has little lifting power," Professor Charles concluded. "In addition, it must be continually heated."

"What would you use instead?" he was asked.

"Hydrogen," Professor Charles said. "It is the lightest gas, and will provide far better lift than hot air."

Hydrogen had been discovered 15 years earlier. However, hydrogen was so thin it escaped through the pores of the bag, whether made of cloth or paper. Professor Charles invented a new fabric of silk coated with rubber. The fabric was both light and strong. Hydrogen gas could not penetrate its surface.

Working quickly, Professor Charles designed and built a man-carrying

The beautiful cathedral St. Pierre graces the countryside in Normandy, France.

hydrogen-filled balloon in less than two months. He invented ways to control the balloon's flight. To make it descend, he opened a valve that released gas, reducing lift. To make it rise, he poured sand from bags, lightening the load. He also supported the passenger basket by a net over the balloon. The net helped spread out the weight.

Professor Charles set the day for his manned flight: December 17, 1783. The people of Paris declared a holiday. They closed their shops. A half million people trooped out to the parade grounds to see the sight.

Professor Charles and a friend who rode with him did not disappoint the crowd. His balloon performed flawlessly. It rose to 1,800 feet. He measured his altitude by means of a barometer.

Professor Charles said to his friend, "The sky belongs to us! What a breath-taking scene!"

About two hours after liftoff, Professor Charles pulled the rope that opened the valve at the top of the balloon. Some of the hydrogen gas escaped and the balloon began settling back to earth.

Shortly after sundown the two men landed in an open field about 25 miles from Paris. His friend stepped from the basket. With the balloon made lighter, it could fly again.

Professor Charles stayed aboard in a solo flight. He enjoyed an unusual spectacle. The gain in altitude made the setting sun visible again. When he landed, he said, "I had the pleasure of seeing the sun set twice on the same day!"

Overlooking the Luberon Valley, Provenance, France.

Jacques Charles proved a skillful and popular lecturer. People flocked to hear about his exploits. He described the balloon flights so perfectly, the audience felt as if they were in the balloon with him. "Nothing can approach the fascinating joy in my spirit as I felt that we were leaving the earth," he said. "It was not a simple pleasure. It was a real joy. I have never seen anything so beautiful in my lifetime!"

Balloons became tools of the military. They made good observation platforms to watch the movement of troops. Balloons also made possible the scientific exploraticn of the upper atmosphere.

In 1804, Joseph Gay-Lussac (GAY-lyoo-SAK) inherited a balloon from Napoleon's army. He loaded the balloon with scientific instruments and began higher and higher flights. In his most daring and dangerous flight, he reached a height of four miles, higher than the tallest peak of the Alps.

The flight nearly cost him his life. The atmosphere becomes colder and thinner with height. In the bitter cold, the air became too thin to supply enough oxygen. Breathing became difficult. His vision blurred. His fingers became too stiff to operate the gas release control. Gay-Lussac fainted. He revived a few minutes later after the balloon lost altitude.

Gay-Lussac did prove that the gases that make up the atmosphere remained the same with height, as did the strength of the earth's magnetic field.

Joseph Gay-Lussac was a French chemist and physicist who was well known for his studies of gases. In 1809, after a balloon ascent he put his knowledge of science together with what he observed and formulated a "law of Gases" that is still used today and called the "Gay-Lussac law."

Despite the feats of daring men such as Jacques Charles and Joseph Gay-Laussac, the balloon proved unsuited in many ways. Another, more important road to the conquest of the skies was to be found by heavier-than-air craft.

Strategic Balloon Exploration

A mere 80 years after Joseph and Jacques Montgolfier launched their first balloon, an American discovered a way to help win the Civil War. A young scientist named Thaddeus Lowe convinced war planners that intelligence-gathering on Confederate positions could be enhanced by using observation balloons.

Lowe's idea did indeed aid the Union, and the illustrations on this page document the work of the U.S. Balloon Corps during the years 1861-65.

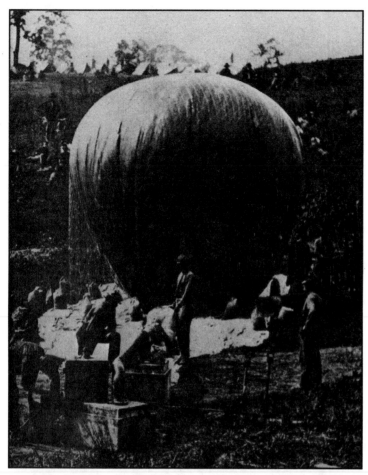

The balloon Intrepid (above and below), June 1862.

The first barge to tow a Civil War observation balloon, in this scene from the James River.

Questions

Exploring by Balloon

Choose A or B to complete the sentence.

1. The first hot air balloons were made by
   - A. sons of famous scientists.
   - B. sons of a paper manufacturer.

2. Hot air rises because it is
   - A. heavier than cold air.
   - B. lighter than cold air.

3. The Montgolfiers built a balloon big enough to carry
   - A. two sheep and a goat.
   - B. two human beings.

4. The first people to rise in a hot air balloon were
   - A. two criminals.
   - B. a young nobleman and his friend.

5. The first balloon flights with human passengers were seen by
   - A. a few dozen people.
   - B. more than a hundred thousand people.

6. Professor Jacques Charles made a balloon that replaced hot air with
   - A. carbon dioxide gas.
   - B. hydrogen gas.

7. Joseph Gay-Lussac took scientific instruments with him in his balloon and went
   - A. across the English channel.
   - B. to a great height.

Thought Question:

8. Describe how Professor Jacques Charles could control the rise and fall of his balloon.

_____

_____

CHAPTER 18

THE AGE OF FLIGHT

People have dreamed of flying since they first watched birds soaring in the sky. The sleek powerful jets we see flying today are the result of those dreams being turned into action.

Balloons are lighter-than-air craft. They float in air because they are lighter than air. Birds, however, are heavier than air, yet they can fly, too.

The first person to study heavier-than-air flight was Leonardo da Vinci. He is best known as the painter of *Mona Lisa* and *The Last Supper*. But he was also a man of science and an inventor. Leonardo lived two centuries before the Montgolfier brothers. In his manuscript, *On the Flight of Birds*, he concluded that if birds could fly, then people could make flying machines, too. Leonardo drew designs of aircraft, and invented the parachute.

Leonardo worked in secret, so how much success he achieved is unknown. But a human being has such a poor power-to-weight ratio, that to fly by flapping wings like the birds is out of the question.

In the late 1800s, Otto Lilienthal (LIL-een-thal) took up the challenge of "air sailing" in Germany.

For 20 years he sketched bird's wings in various positions. No one before had studied birds so intently. Otto Lilienthal was the first person to realize that heavy birds, like storks, took off into the wind. He wrote a book, *Bird Flight as the Basis of the Flying Art*.

With the help of his brother Gustave, he constructed a glider with wings like those of birds. Lilienthal's machine seemed small and delicate. Its wings were only 18 feet across. He didn't flap the wings to take off. Instead, he threw himself into the wind from a height.

The place in Germany where Lilienthal lived had few suitable places to launch himself into the air. In 1893 a canal was being dug near his house. Otto and Gustave Lilienthal persuaded the canal builder to pile

Leonardo da Vinci was not only an artist, but he also had a brilliant scientific mind. He believed that if birds could fly, then people could make flying machines. He filled notebooks with his ideas and sketched how he thought they would work. He also wrote about anatomy, physics, optics, biology, and hydraulics.

Leonardo had a deep faith in Christ and the Scriptures. His painting, "The Last Supper," has blessed the hearts of Christians over the centuries.

up the dirt in the middle of a field. This made a fine jumping-off place 50 feet high.

Otto Lilienthal controlled the aircraft by shifting his weight around. He learned how to turn, to hover, and to soar — to rise above his launch point. During five years, Otto Lilienthal made more than 2,000 successful flights.

Then in 1896 he tested a new design. A sudden gust of wind tipped his batlike glider. It side-slipped into a fall. Otto Lilienthal died of injuries suffered in the crash. As he lay dying, he gasped to his brother, "Sacrifices must be made."

During this same time, Dr. Samuel P. Langley worked on a flying machine. He was the scientist in charge of the Smithsonian Institution. The Institution is a combination museum, library, and scientific laboratory. It is much like the library at Alexandria that Eratosthenes ran more than 2,000 years ago.

Dr. Langley spent six years and more than $100,000 to make three machines. He launched his airplanes from the top of a houseboat on the Potomac River near Washington, D.C. Each time the airplanes crashed into the water.

Newspaper editors took Dr. Langley to task for his foolish waste of taxpayers money. Langley was the world's foremost aeronautical engineer. Most people thought that if he couldn't make a flying machine, then no one could.

Orville Wright and his older brother Wilbur started the Wright Cycle Company in 1893 in Dayton, Ohio. They earned their living by building and selling bicycles of their own design. The Wright brothers were largely self-taught. They were sons of a minister. They lived upright lives and neither

smoked nor drank. They always dressed neatly, and even wore business suits when tinkering in their bicycle shop.

The Wright brothers read of the tragic death of Otto Lilienthal. The story turned their thoughts back to a boyhood interest in mechanical birds.

They read the scientific papers written by Lilienthal and Langley. When Orville and Wilbur repeated the experiments, they discovered errors in the standard air pressure tables. Lilienthal and Langley based their designs upon incorrect information.

The Wrights began afresh. They built a wind tunnel and completely recomputed air

Samuel P. Langley was an astronomer and pioneer in the early design of airplanes. He devoted much of his research in astronomy to the study of solar radiation.

pressures for wings of various lengths, widths, and curves.

The Wrights built a five-foot model and flew it at the end of a string like a kite.

The first bicycle (1690) was vastly different from the sleek racing models we ride today. It was only a wooden beam with wheels attached. The bicycle shown above with the large front wheel was popular in the 1870s. By the time of the Wright brothers, bicycle design had come a long way! They now had handlebars for steering, brakes, seats, and rubber tires. The brothers worked in their bicycle shop and dreamed of flying.

The winds around Dayton weren't reliable enough for them. They asked the Weather Bureau to suggest a better site. The Weather Bureau recommended the coast of North Carolina — the sea breezes there were particularly constant and dependable.

When summer ended and the bicycle season slacked off, the brothers packed their things and traveled by train to North Carolina. The site offered good winds, low sandy hills, and no trees to accidentally crash into.

The first problem was to learn how to control the aircraft and keep it balaced during flight. Shifting the pilot's weight around, as Otto Lilienthal did, wouldn't keep it level during sudden gusts of wind.

Orville observed how buzzards righted themselves when rocked to one side by crosswinds. Looking through binoculars he saw that the buzzard dropped one wing and lifted the other. He noticed a tiny twist of the feathers at the tips of the wings. As feathers went up on one side, feathers twisted down on the other side.

Here was something that Lilienthal himself had overlooked. By twisting the wing tips, the pilot could control the airplane.

After proving the design in a tethered kite, the two brothers cut loose the ropes and took turns making gliding flights. Orville became such an expert glider pilot he stayed in the air for nine minutes, riding along the updraft from the low sand dunes. This record for unpowered flight was not broken for ten years.

Their first goal — controlled flight — was a reality. Now they turned to the second goal — powered flight. Sustained flight would only be possible with a lightweight and powerful engine.

The airplane model in the museum barely resembles the planes we have today. Despite its clumsy appearance, this airplane had one feature not shared by those before it. It could get off the ground!

They calculated the power needed to propel their aircraft. They mailed their specifications to companies that made gasoline engines. The replies came back. An engine like the Wright brothers needed simply couldn't be made.

Orville and Wilbur built their own engine. They began with an automobile engine and substituted aluminum parts wherever possible. The four-cylinder water-cooled engine weighed 240 pounds and delivered 12 horsepower. It was unusually light for the power it delivered.

The airplane, including engine and pilot, weighed only 750 pounds. The time had come to make the first trial flight. The Wright brothers announced their test in the local newspaper. Only five people turned out on the cold, windswept slopes of Kill Devil Hill near Kitty Hawk to watch the Wright brothers attempt the first powered and controlled flight of a heavier-than-air machine.

By the time the Wrights flew, only a few regions of the earth had not been visited by scientist-explorers. North and South Poles were still to be explored, as were a few of the most remote jungles, deserts, and mountains.

The site of the first successful flight in a motor-powered airplane is now the Wright Brothers National Memorial. The monument (left) is seen on the hill behind the brothers plaque (bottom). The monument can be seen from a great distance and is still buffeted by winds like those that blew on the day they made history.

Shortly before their attempt, Dr. Langley's aircraft crashed for the third time. He gave up his experiments. The *New York Times* concluded, "Man will not fly for a thousand years."

Nine days later, on December 17, 1903, the Wrights made not one, but four, successful flights. In the longest one, Orville Wright piloted the *Flyer* a distance of 850 feet. He stayed in the air for almost a minute. Their expenses for the eight years of trying came to $1,000.

Airplanes changed the way scientists went about explorations. From then on, a small party would trek to the site of interest and clear a landing strip. Then airplanes would ferry in scientists, supplies, and scientific equipment.

Richard E. Byrd was the first person to make extensive use of airplanes to aid exploration. He was from the famous Byrd family of Virginia. He always wanted to explore. At age 12, he made a trip on his own around the world.

The largest blank area on any map was the continent of Antarctica at the South Pole. Five million square miles of uninhabited land waited to be explored.

With backing from private donors, Richard Byrd organized in 1928 an expedition to Antarctica. More than 30 scientists went with him. They established a base named Little America on the eastern edge of the Ross Ice Shelf.

Richard Byrd and two other men flew to the South Pole and back. The one-day trip covered 1,600 miles. Two years earlier, he'd flown over the North Pole. Richard Byrd became the first person to fly over both the North and South Poles.

In 1934 Byrd spent five months alone in a hut at a tiny base 125 miles south of Little America. No human being had ever wintered on that frozen continent. He had the entire Antarctic continent to himself. Richard E. Byrd was certainly the loneliest person on earth.

In 1939 Byrd headed another airplane expedition. He and the scientists with him mapped the frozen expanse of Antarctic from the air. More than anyone else he unfolded Antarctica to the world of science.

Richard Byrd is only one example of how flying opened the inaccessible regions of the world. As another example, consider the case of an American adventurer and pilot named James Angel. An oil company looked for likely places to drill for oil in Venezuela, in South America. They hired him as pilot.

One day he was flying his plane in southeastern Venezuela, over the Guiana

Richard E. Byrd graduated from the U.S. Naval Academy in 1912. By 1930 he had earned the rank of rear admiral. He had an exciting career and was awarded the Medal of Honor for the first flight over the North Pole.

highlands. It was the least-known and least-developed part of South America. James Angel followed a river, the Rio Churun. Suddenly the river plunged over a sheer cliff. It separated into brilliant white sheets. The water fell, and fell, and fell. The water disappeared into boiling mists at the bottom. The water fell 3,232 feet — more than a half mile.

Quite unexpectedly, James Angel had discovered the highest waterfall in the world. Of course, the sight was named after him — Angel Falls.

Questions

The Age of Flight

Choose A or B to complete the sentence.

1. People pointed to birds as examples of
   - A. lighter-than-air craft.
   - B. heavier-than-air craft.

2. Leonardo da Vinci invented
   - A. the parachute.
   - B. the first powered airplane.

3. Otto Lilienthal died
   - A. from a mishap with a glider.
   - B. while sailing a boat.

4. Dr. Samuel P. Langley was a scientist
   - A. but his airplanes crashed into the Potomac River.
   - B. who made the first successful airplanes.

5. The Wright Brothers
   - A. were employed at the Smithsonian Institution.
   - B. manufactured bicycles.

6. Who concluded that "Man will not fly for a thousand years":
   - A. the *New York Times*.
   - B. the U. S. Weather Service.

7. Richard Byrd used airplanes to explore
   - A. high in the atmosphere.
   - B. the North and South Polar regions.

8. Angel Falls are given that name
   - A. because the water looks like the wings of an angel.
   - B. because the falls were discovered by a pilot named James Angel.

Thought Questions:

9. What does controlled flight mean? What does powered flight mean?

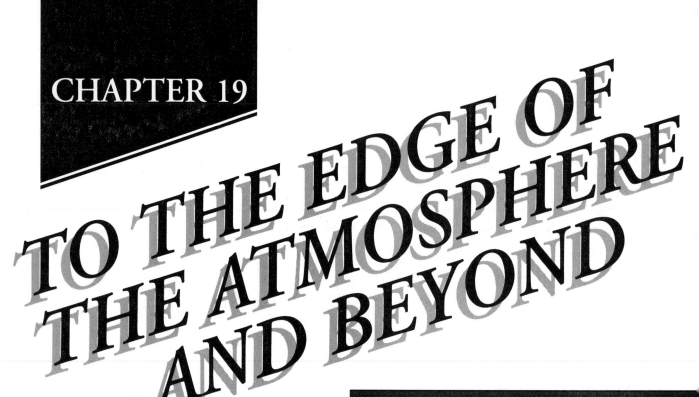

CHAPTER 19

TO THE EDGE OF THE ATMOSPHERE — AND BEYOND

Robert Hutchings Goddard dreamed of rocket flight, not only into the upper atmosphere, but to the moon and planets. Once, as a young boy, he trimmed dead branches from a cherry tree behind a barn on his grandfather's farm. He climbed the tall tree. As he worked, he daydreamed about the chances of sending a rocket to the moon.

This was in 1899, the same year that Henry Ford began manufacturing his automobile. It would be another eight years before Robert Goddard himself rode in an automobile. The automobile hit a breathtaking speed of 15 miles an hour.

Night launches at Kennedy Space Center light up the sky for miles. Launches are announced in advance and often crowds of thousands gather to watch the space shuttle lift off.

Robert Goddard suffered several bouts with illnesses. Once, doctors detected tuberculosis in both lungs. They feared he wouldn't live. Robert Goddard did survive, although the medical problems left him far behind children his own age at school.

Robert Goddard had many hobbies. He liked to draw, to write stories, and to play musical instruments. He sang in the choir at the church he attended. He also dreamed about the future.

As one example of his daring imagination, he thought up the idea for a high speed railway line. Passengers rode in pressurized train cars carried through a large vacuum pipe. Without air resistance, the train whisked passengers from Boston to New York in ten minutes, rather than four hours. He called the idea "Traveling in 1950." Of course, by 1950, it *still* took four hours to travel between the two cities.

Robert looked into the problems of rocket flight. He read books on the atmosphere, on the theory of flight, on astronomy, and on anything that had to do with high altitude.

The Chinese invented the first rockets sometime in the 1200s. These rockets were nothing more than dressed up fireworks, like those used today during Fourth of July celebrations. A rocket gains forward thrust by shooting out hot gases in the opposite direction. The hot gases of the Chinese rockets came from burning gun powder.

During the War of 1812 the British fired rockets in the bombardment of Fort McHenry. Francis Scott Key was held prisoner aboard a British ship during the battle. He wrote a poem that later became the United States' national anthem. One of the lines of "The Star Spangled Banner" describes the "rocket's red glare."

Though his work was almost ignored in his own country during his lifetime, Robert Hutchings Goddard, laid the foundation for modern space exploration.

Dreaming alone is not enough. Success requires knowledge and skill, too. Robert Goddard immediately began to study harder. He graduated from Worcester Polytechnic Institute at the top of his class.

In 1914 he wrote a summary of his rocket researches. The report, "A Method of Reaching Extreme Altitudes," came to the attention of the Smithsonian. They gave him

$5,000 for further experiments. The report itself didn't get published until 1919.

Robert Goddard invented the first of a new type of rocket engine, one that burned kerosene and liquid oxygen. He built rocket motors in his laboratory and tried them out. Each successful rocket test required hard work, attention to detail, and careful planning.

He built a complete rocket in 1926. On a cold March morning of that year he set up the rocket in a field outside Worcester, Massachusetts. Snow covered the field. The sky was clear and the wind didn't blow, and that was what mattered.

Only a couple of Goddard's friends came to watch the flight. Esther, his wife, took pictures of him standing by the little rocket. Her photographs of this experiment, and later ones, would be the only visual record of his pioneering efforts.

Robert Goddard lit the rocket with a blow torch. The flimsy contraption shot away from the frame which held it. The rocket flew to a landing 200 feet away. It was the first successful flight of a modern rocket.

When Robert Goddard spoke of rocket flight to "extreme altitudes" he meant into orbit around the earth and even to the moon.

When people learned of his plan to send rockets into space, they called Goddard's work a silly idea. Canadian astronomer Professor J. W. Campbell of the University of Alberta said, "Rocket flight would appear to be more than 100 years in the future." A high-ranking American scientist said, "In my opinion such a thing is impossible for many years."

Human beings first set foot on the moon on July 20, 1969. If Goddard had still been alive he would have been pleased to see the scientific uses of his rocket discoveries.

The first view of the earth from the moon was an amazing sight.

An editorial in the *New York Times* gleefully pointed out that a rocket motor wouldn't operate in the emptiness of space. "The motor would have nothing to push against," the newspaper said.

Robert Goddard had long ago settled that question. While still in college he pumped air out of a long pipe and fired a small rocket motor inside. The engine did work in a vacuum.

Robert Goddard continued his experiments. His fourth liquid fuel rocket was 11 feet long. Packed into its nose was a barometer to measure air pressure, a thermometer to read the temperature, and a small camera

to photograph the flight. It was the first rocket to carry a scientific payload.

Unfortunately, the rocket flight started a grass fire. Farmers complained that the terrific roar from the engine disturbed their cows. The whole neighborhood complained and called the police. Officials ordered Robert Goddard to put an end to his experiments.

Charles Lindbergh, who had become a national hero by flying the Atlantic alone, arranged for Goddard to receive $50,000.

Robert and Esther immediately moved to Roswell, New Mexico. There they found the isolation they sought. They built a permanent launching tower. For the next ten years,

Robert Goddard carried out experiments which lead to success after success.

By 1935, Dr. Goddard's rockets had reached 7,500 feet at a speed of over 500 miles per hour. During these years he received more than 200 patents for his rocket work. Yet, his work was largely ignored — in the United States, anyway.

In Germany, it was a different matter. Rocket scientists poured over the patents. His scientific papers were read with keen interest.

The leading German rocket expert was Wernher von Braun. In 1930, he had joined the German Society for Space Travel. This group of amateurs built and tested rockets.

In all, the amateur group fired 85 rockets. One reached an altitude of a mile.

In 1933 Adolf Hitler came into power. The German army took over the rocket program. To his horror, Wernher von Braun saw his group forced to build rockets as weapons of war. By 1944 the deadly V-2 was perfected. By then it was clear that Hitler would be defeated.

The Gestapo, the feared German police, arrested Wernher von Braun and threw him into prison. They accused him of being more interested in space travel than in building V-2s (which happened to be true). The Gestapo released him when Allied forces invaded France.

This photo of White Sands National Park in New Mexico shows why this area was a good selection for a supersecret testing sight for early missile development. They didn't have any neighbors for miles and anyone trying to sneak up on the installation could be seen from a far distance.

Then disaster of another sort struck. A car in which Wernher rode crashed into a railroad embankment and burst into flames. Wernher forced open the door and pulled the driver to safety. At the hospital they found that Wernher's left arm was broken in two places and the shoulder shattered. The doctor set the arm in a cast, but he shook his head. He doubted if the arm would heal properly.

Wernher moved the rocket group away from the fighting, to Oberammergau, a little village in the Bavarian Alps.

Wernher's broken arm became infected. High fever gripped his body. Friends sent for the local doctor. But what could a simple country doctor do that a well-equipped hospital could not do?

Unexpected good fortune saved von Braun's life. The little town was a ski resort. The town doctor had set more broken bones than any other doctor in Germany. The doctor removed the cast. With gentle fingers he examined the red and inflamed flesh. "The arm will have to be rebroken and reset."

Because of the war shortages, the doctor had to work without a painkiller. Wernher gritted his teeth and let the doctor go ahead. This time it healed properly.

Wernher von Braun, a German-American engineer, is best known for his development of the liquid-fuel rocket.

When the war ended, von Braun and his group of rocket experts surrendered to the Americans. Again he called for rockets to be put to peaceful purposes. From the time he gave his heart to the Lord at age 14, Wernher von Braun held strong religious beliefs. He said, "As we study our equations and sail our space ships, we must always remember that our first concern is for man himself. Our science must increase man's blessings."

The German rocket scientists moved to White Sands, the Army's proving ground in New Mexico. It was only a few miles from Roswell, New Mexico, where Robert Goddard had built his miniature space center.

Wernher von Braun and his band of experts repaired captured V-2s and test fired them.

The V-2 was 46 feet long and 5-1/2 feet across. It weighed 13 tons when fully loaded. The V-2 burned alcohol for fuel and carried liquid oxygen to make the alcohol burn. Its payload was about 2,000 pounds. In wartime the missile carried explosives.

But the payload could be a scientific package — or even another rocket. In 1949 a smaller American-made WAC Corporal rocket was fitted to the top of a V-2. This

Science fiction writers often wrote about the precautions that an astronaut would need to take while in space. The astronauts are highly trained. They wear space suits that have been specially designed for the harsh conditions of space.

two-stage rocket attained a speed of 5,150 miles per hour. It soared to a height of 250 miles above the earth. It measured electrically charged particles in the upper atmosphere.

Despite these successes, the American government still was not particularly interested in rockets.

Wernher began work on a project he had dreamed about for years. He wrote a book, *The Mars Project*, in which he explained how mankind could go into space and explore the planets.

Nobody seemed interested. Most people considered the whole idea of space travel too fantastic. In all, 18 publishers turned down the book.

Frequently he was asked, "But what good is space flight?"

His standard answer recalled the story of Michael Faraday, the English scientist who lived in the 1800s. When someone asked Faraday the value of electricity, he responded, "What use is a newborn baby?"

Wernher said, "Through a closer look at creation, we ought to gain a knowledge of the Creator, and a greater sense of man's responsibilities to God will come into focus."

At last the University of Illinois Press agreed to publish his book.

In 1950 Wernher von Braun and his family moved to the southern town of Huntsville, Alabama. He decided to become an American citizen. He and his family attended church regularly and took part in church activities. Soon, their German chocolate cake became a favorite dessert at church picnics. Wernher von Braun became an American citizen in 1955.

Interest in space travel suddenly increased in 1957. The International Geophysical Year, or IGY, began on July 1 and extended until December 1958. The "year" was actually 18 months. It was a time set aside for scientists to explore all aspects of the earth.

The Soviet Union announced its plans to orbit a satellite during the IGY. Most people, especially Americans, discounted that story, thinking the Soviet rocket program to be far behind the American program.

On October 4, 1957, Wernher von Braun was at a dinner at Redstone Arsenal with the Secretary of Defense. Suddenly the public-relations officer dashed to their table. Breathlessly, he announced that the Soviets had successfully orbited a satellite.

Then, less than a month later, the Soviets launched yet another satellite. *Sputnik II* carried a payload of more than 1,100 pounds.

The United States government frantically ordered the navy to rush ahead with an untried rocket named Vanguard. Unfortunately, Vanguard exploded on the launching pad. American hopes for a satellite of their own seemed in ruins.

Government leaders called von Braun, who worked for the army, to Washington. "What can you do?" they said.

He said, "We can use the equipment on hand and build a satellite-carrying rocket in 60 days."

The space shuttle, Atlantis, makes a safe landing. The shuttle will be thoroughly checked for damage of any kind and then made ready for another trip into space.

Von Braun's army group placed the first American satellite, Explorer I, into orbit on January 31, 1958. Explorer I radioed back data showing that a radiation belt surrounded the earth. The earth's magnetic field captured charged particles streaming out from the sun. The radiation belt had not even been suspected before Explorer I.

The first object to be explored by rockets into space was not the moon or one of the other planets. Instead, the earth itself came under the most detailed and revealing study. For the first time, the earth as a whole could be seen.

Earth's landscape is graceful and beautiful, but no one knew how beautiful until astronauts returned from space with color photographs of the earth. The photographs showed a planet of blue-green oceans, misty clouds, and land that ranged from the dark green of wooded mountains to the fiery red of deserts.

Throughout the space program, astronauts returned to earth with an unusual experience. Somehow the view of earth from

space made them look at it in an entirely new way.

Astronaut Jim Irwin of Apollo 15 described it this way, "Seeing earth (from space) has to change a man, has to make a man appreciate the creation of God and the love of God."

Scientists have explored all levels of the earth, from the upper atmosphere to the depths of the ocean. No other planet has frozen tundras, steamy rain forests, hot deserts, snow capped mountains, green valleys, sandy beaches, cool caves, and fiery volcanos. Of all the planets, only the earth has such endless variety.

Earth is an interesting planet. It is the only planet where snow can fall, the only planet where tides stir up a restless sea, the only planet with weather that is varied and beautiful.

What makes the earth so special? The Psalmist said, "The sea is his, and he made it: and his hands formed the dry land" (Ps. 95:5). And in Psalm 33:5, "The earth is full of the goodness of the Lord."

Our world is a beautiful planet, unlike anything else in the solar system. As Moses said, "As truly as I live, all the earth shall be filled with the glory of the Lord" (Num. 14:21).

What did Wernher von Braun think of the success of his rocket program? "Because of the wonderful things it has done for society, we are tempted to place too high a value on science."

He said, "We must consider God as Creator of the universe and master of everything. Astronomy and space exploration are teaching us that the good Lord is a much greater Lord, and the master of a greater kingdom."

"In the beginning God created the heaven and the earth" (Gen. 1:1).

Questions

To the Edge of the Atmosphere — and Beyond

Choose A or B to complete the sentence.

1. Rockets go forward because they

    A. overcome the law of gravity.

    B. shoot hot gases out the back.

2. A photograph was taken of Robert Goddard's first rocket flight by

    A. a newspaper reporter.

    B. his wife.

3. Robert Goddard

    A. proved that rockets would work in the vacuum of space.

    B. didn't sent rockets into space because he didn't think they would fly in a vacuum.

4. Robert Goddard's papers were read with keen interest by

    A. American scientists.

    B. German scientists.

5. Wernher von Braun's book titled *The Mars Project* was

    A. eagerly purchased by a major New York publisher.

    B. turned down by 18 publishers.

6. The first country to put an artificial satellite into orbit around the earth was

    A. Japan.

    B. the Soviet Union.

7. The first American satellite was put into orbit by a group led by

    A. Robert Goddard.

    B. Wernher von Braun.

Thought Question:

8. How did space travel change human beings' understanding of the earth?

_____

_____

CHAPTER 20

EXPLORING IN TODAY'S WORLD

Cavers decending into Sotano de las Golondrinas cave in Mexico.

Much of the earth was unknown to the Romans. Even the parts they did know about were largely unexplored. Mapmakers pictured about half the Roman world as blank areas. They labeled the blanks *terra incognito*. The term means "hidden land." With time, explorers filled in the unknown areas.

Today, no spot on the globe is hidden or unknown. Yet, exploration has not ceased. Learning about the world is as important today as it was 2,000 years ago.

Exploration is not merely the quest for new lands. It is the quest for knowledge. Within the earth, within the seas, and beyond the earth to the moon and planets, the quest for knowledge goes on.

Thrilling sagas of adventure are being written today. Discoveries as important as any of those described in this book await people of talent and daring.

Perhaps the next chapter in the story of exploration will be written by you.

There are "worlds" left to explore!

Below the earth

Caver in the Guadalupe Mountains of New Mexico looking at an old waterline below ground.

Beneath the sea

Scuba diver in the Pacific Ocean.

And into space

Space shuttle launch at Kennedy Space Center, Florida

BIBLIOGRAPHY

Asimov, Isaac, *Asimov's Biographical Encyclopedia of Science and Technology*, 2nd Revised Edition (Garden City, NY: Doubleday & Co., Inc., 1982).

Bailey, Bernadine Freeman, *Famous Modern Explorers* (New York City, NY: Dodd, Mead & Co., 1963).

Bishop, Richard W., *From Kite to Kitty Hawk* (New York City, NY: Thomas Y. Crowell Co., 1958).

Brett, Bernard, Ed., *Explorers and Exploring* (Baltimore, MD: Penguin Books, Inc., 1973).

Briggs, Peter, *Rivers in the Sea* (New York City, NY: Weybright and Talley, Inc., 1969).

Davies, Stella, *Exploring the World* (New York City, NY: Roy Publishers, Inc., 1965).

Day, A. Grove, *Explorers of the Pacific* (New York City, NY: Duell, Sloan and Pearce, 1966).

Graves, Charles P., *A World Explorer: Marco Polo* (Champaign, IL: Garrard Publishing Co., 1963).

Komroff, Manuel, *Marco Polo* (New York City, NY: Julian Messer, Inc., 1952).

Lucas, Mary Seymour, *Vast Horizons* (New York City, NY: The Viking Press, 1943).

Morris, Henry M., *Men of Science, Men of God* (Green Forest, AR: Master Books, 1982).

Neal, Harry Edward, *The Mystery of Time* (New York City, NY: Julian Messner, 1966).

Verral, Charles Spain, *Robert Goddard: Father of the Space Age* (Englewood Cliffs, NJ: Prentice-Hall, Inc., 1963).

Weiner, Jonathan, *Planet Earth* (New York City, NY: Bantam Books, Inc., 1985).

INDEX

Illustration/Photo Credits

t-top, b-bottom, c-left, r-right, a-all illustrations on page

Planet Art Antique Maps: 1, 4, 16, 24, 28, 32, 38, 76, 100

Cartesia Map Art: 5b, 7, 11, 14, 27, 29, 34, 42a, 58, 66, 79, 86, 88a, 90, 91a, 103, 104b, 107, 108t, 110

Ron Height (illustrations): 8, 10, 12, 13, 18, 20, 25, 26, 30, 33, 36, 41, 53, 54, 55, 63, 67, 70, 71, 72, 77, 78, 83, 84, 92, 104t, 116, 117, 119a, 120, 122, 123, 127, 131, 136, 140, 143

Corel Stock Photography Library: 17, 21a, 22, 47, 49a, 52, 56, 62, 64, 68, 86b, 88a, 90, 91*a, 94, 95, 97, 101, 102a, 105a, 106, 108b, :113, 121, 129, 130, 132a, 134, 142, 144—150, 153—153

Jeanene Tiner (photography): 2, 57, 69, 111, 114, 128, 138t, 139a

Corel Clipart: 3, 4, 45, 46, 60, 135, 138

Zedcore Design Galley: 5t, 35, 39, 40, 73, 112a, 126, 137a

Expert Software Photo CD Gallery #2: 48a

Mountain High Maps: 82

Earl and Bonita Snellenberger: 96

Suggested Reading List

Clanin, Gloria, *In the Days of Noah*, (Green Forest, Arkansas: Master Books, 1996), 80 pp.

Gish, Duane T., *Dinosaurs By Design*, (Green Forest, Arkansas: Master Books, 1992), 88 pp.

Ham, Ken and Mally, *D is for Dinosaur*, (Green Forest, Arkansas: Master Books, 1991), 123 pp.

Morris, John D., *Noah's Ark and the Ararat Adventure*, (Green Forest, Arkansas: Master Books, 1988), 64 pp.

Morris, John D., And Ham, Ken, *What Really Happened to the Dinosaurs?*, (Green Forest, Arkansas: Master Books, 1990), 32 pp.

Oard, Michael and Beverly, *Life in the Great Ice Age*, (Green Forest, Arkansas: Master Books, 1993), 72 pp.

Oard, Michael, *The Weather Book*, (Green Forest, Arkansas: Master Books, 1997), 80 pp.

Parker, Gary, *Dry Bones and Other Fossils*, (Green Forest, Arkansas: Master Books, 1995), 80 pp.

Answers to Chapter Questions

Chapter 1
1. A. knowledge about the earth
2. B. Egypt
3. A. the greatest library in the ancient world
4. B. calculate the distance around the earth
5. B. small
6. answer varies, intelligence is the faculty of thought and reason, knowledge is specific information about something
7. answer varies, although not as knowledgeable, many were as intelligent
8. answer varies, he revealed knowledge about the size of the earth

Chapter 2
1. Phoenicians
2. answer varies, Ursa Major, big bear, great bear and its cubs, sky chariot
3. any three of cedar, cloth, purple dye, papyrus, ivory, ebony, silk, spices
4. he described the sun at noon as being in the northern half of the sky, which is true for observers in the Southern Hemisphere in summer
5. The Mediterranean
6. answer varies, travel on the Atlantic was more dangerous than on the Mediterranean Sea, people around the coast of the Mediterranean thought of themselves as civilized and everyone else as barbarians

Chapter 3
1. B. numerous small kingdoms
2. B. threw strangers into prison
3. B. Kublai Khan
4. A. ambassador
5. A. a fleet of sailing ships
6. B. 24 years
7. B. a jail cell
8. answer varies, asbestos is a mineral that appears to be a fabric and does not burn, coal is an organic material that appears to be a rock but does burn
9. answer varies, his descriptions of China often included the phrase "millions"
10. answer varies, to give variety to the taste of food and conceal the fact that the food might be spoiled

Chapter 4
1. A. latitude
2. A. finding their longitude
3. A. go to a chapel to pray
4. A. east
5. answer varies, because of being transported from a greater distance and taxes
6. answer varies, a legendary Christian leader in Africa who was separated from Europe by the Arab empire
7. answer varies, court affairs in Lisbon constantly interrupted his studies
8. answer varies, because of his single minded determination to improve navigation and find a route to India

Chapter 5
1. B. studied the best maps, charts and books, including those of Ptolemy and Marco Polo
2. B. fell to his knees and gave thanks to God
3. B. 'The Saviour'
4. B. sailor
5. B. in chains
6. B. Amerigo Vespucius, an Italian navigator
7. answer varies, because of his incorrect information that the earth was 18,000 miles around, not the correct distance of about 25,000 miles
8. answer varies, they didn't expect to see ships or men again

Chapter 6
1. B. a Viking
2. A. Greenland
3. A. the North American coast
4. A. a change in climate
5. B. South America
6. A. storm-tossed they test a sea captain's skill
7. B. he died during the fighting between two native tribes in the Philippines
8. answer varies, they did not make the discovery known to the rest of the Europe
9. answer varies, knowledge is also needed of winds, ocean currents, earth's magnetic fields, tide tables, also needed are accurate clocks

Chapter 7
1. gentle - a. cat's paw
2. dry - d. Santa Ana
3. rain - c. monsoon
4. windstorm - g. willy-willy
5. whirlwind - b. dust devil

6. tornado - e. twister
7. hurricane - f. typhoon
8. B. rotation of the earth
9. A. convection

Chapter 8
1. A. did not know about tides
2. B. tides
3. B. because of winds and weather conditions
4. B. Isaac Newton
5. B. the most important science book ever published
6. A. Bible study
7. B. the sun
8. answer varies, tides are not directly under the moon, friction along the ocean's floor, they are affected by the sun, the shape of the land they strike, and weather conditions
9. answer varies, tides change levels of shallow bays so ships can enter, and they provide power

Chapter 9
1. B. putting an iron object too near the compass needle
2. B. William Gilbert
3. B. several hundred miles from one another
4. B. but weak
5. sudden changes in compass readings (they produce the northern lights, too, but not the northern lights alone)
6. answer varies, a dip compass is mounted to point up and down, when taken to the north magnetic pole it points down rather than up to the North Star

Chapter 10
1. 0
2. 24
3. 360
4. 10
5. Hezekiah - f. prayed for a longer life
6. Christopher Columbus - c. had no accurate clock on his voyages
7. Galileo - b. discovered the principle of the pendulum
8. Christian Huygens - e. made the first pendulum clock
9. John Harrison - d. made the first accurate clock for sea voyages
10. William Bligh - a. carried a copy of Number Four on *The Bounty*

11. answer varies, local time is measured by the position of the sun at a particular location, Greenwich time is the time measured by the position of the sun in Greenwich, England

Chapter 11
1. B. not expected to work
2. A. Benjamin Franklin
3. A. the Gulf Stream
4. B. temperature differences
5. B. the Bible
6. answer varies, they thought they were wiser than the simple American fishermen and ignored their advice
7. answer varies, currents transport oxygen rich water from the surface to deep trenches, England is warmer because of the Gulf Stream, the cold Humboldt current prevents moisture from evaporating as readily and parts of South America are deserts, the temperature of parts of California and Florida are moderated by being close to the ocean

Chapter 12
1. litho - c. prefix meaning "stone"
2. hydro - d. prefix meaning "water"
3. atmosphere - e. the sphere of gas
4. Himalayas mountain range - g. a wrinkle in the crust of the earth
5. Moho discontinuity - b. dividing line between mantle and crust
6. bathysphere - f. William Beebe's ship for deep sea diving
7. Marianas trench - a. deepest part of the ocean
8. answers vary, by shock (sound) waves caused by earthquakes and artificial explosions, by drilling into the earth, and by studying material brought up by volcanoes
9. answer varies, Gasoline is heavier than water and a tank of gasoline gives the bathyscaphe lift. Iron is heavier than water and causes it to sink. By releasing iron pellets, the ship will rise

Chapter 13
1. B. Greenland
2. A. a series of world-wide disasters
3. B. move like slow rivers
4. A. melting glaciers
5. A. get outside and look at it carefully

Chapter 14
1. Nile
2. Yangtze
3. Nile
4. Amazon
5. Yangtze
6. Amazon
7. Yangtze
8. Amazon
9. Nile
10. Nile
11. Amazon
12. Nile
13. answer varies, a river is great not merely by the volume of its flow nor its length, but by its importance for its economic benefit as a source of water, transportation and food to the people who live along its banks

Chapter 15
1. A. Hernando de Soto
2. A. land drained by rivers that flow into the Mississippi from the west
3. B. Rocky Mountains
4. B. the third longest river in the world
5. A. William Henry Jackson
6. Answer varies, United States Representatives and Senators were influenced by the photographs that the spectacular region actually existed and should be protected for all people
7. Answer varies, hot springs, above ground rock formations similar to those in caves, colorful mud pots, waterfalls, colorful canyon, a petrified forest, mountain of obsidian glass, geysers, plant and animal life

Chapter 16
1. A. atmospheric pressure
2. B. measures air pressure
3. A. barometer that measures height above sea level
4. B. less
5. B. against the pull of two teams of horses
6. A. follows laws of science
7. answer varies, a gathering of scientists in England in the 1600s who met and exchanged ideas about the latest discoveries in science, the invisible college later became the Royal Society of London
8. answer varies, Robert Boyle developed the improved design, paid for its construction, and did experiments with it

Chapter 17
1. B. sons of a paper manufacturer
2. B. lighter (less dense) than cold air
3. B. two human beings
4. B. a young nobleman and his friend
5. B. more than a hundred thousand people
6. B. hydrogen gas
7. B. to a great height
8. answer varies, pouring sand from bags while in flight made the balloon lighter and it rose, releasing some of the hydrogen gas caused it to descend

Chapter 18
1. B. heavier-than-air craft
2. A. the parachute
3. A. from a mishap with a glider
4. A. but his airplanes crashed into the Potomac River
5. B. manufactured bicycles
6. A. the New York Times newspaper
7. B. the North and South Polar regions
8. B. because the falls were discovered by a pilot named James Angel
9. answers varies, in controlled flight the pilot can gain and lose altitude and change direction, in powered flight an engine provides thrust and allows the airplane to take off at ground level

Chapter 19
1. B. shoot hot gases out the back
2. B. his wife
3. A. proved that rockets would work in the vacuum of space
4. B. German scientists
5. B. was turned down by 18 publishers
6. B. the Soviet Union
7. B. Wernher von Braun
8. answer varies, "Seeing earth (from space) has to change a man, has to make a man appreciate the creation of God and the love of God." -- Jim Irwin. The earth is revealed as a special creation quite unlike anything else in the solar system

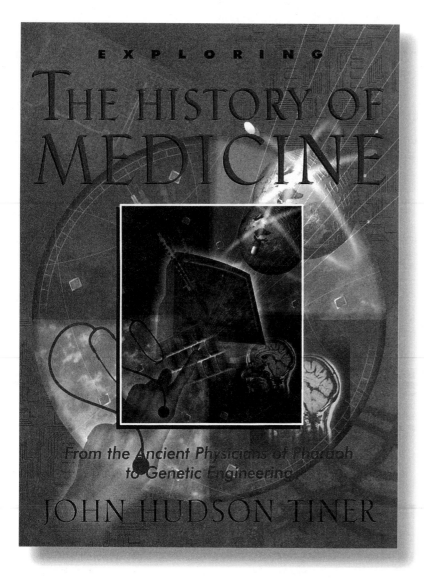

EXPLORING THE WORLD OF CHEMISTRY

JOHN HUDSON TINER

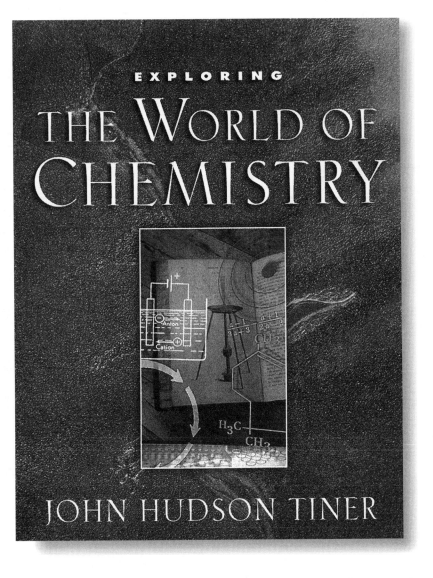

From the search to make gold to the latest advances in silicon microchips, *Exploring Chemistry* takes the reader on an exciting tour of the major achievements of chemistry. Each chapter contains vivid descriptions, exciting action and stirring biographies. Chapters are packed with illustrations, end of chapter questions and a thorough index.

Advances in chemistry are described through the lives of the chemists who made the exciting discoveries. The fascinating breakthroughs in chemistry come alive, providing students with an educational and entertaining look at the discoveries of chemistry.

The chapters focus on individuals who made chemical discoveries that changed the world. Robert Boyle, John Dalton, Michael Faraday and many others were outspoken in their Christian beliefs.

The book is prepared for the home-school market and can serve as a textbook and reading resource. Parents can share it with young children through read-aloud. Later, students can revisit the material for a more in-depth study.

THE ASTRONOMY BOOK

DR. JONATHAN HENRY

The second book in the highly successful "Wonders of Creation" series, The Astronomy Book soars through the solar system targeting middle-school through junior-high levels. The reader will acquire a wealth of knowledge on subjects such as supernovas, red shift, facts about planets, and much more. Enhanced with dozens of color photos and illustrations (including NASA shots), this book gives educators and students a Christian-based look at the awesomeness of the heavens

Abbreviated Table of Contents

$15.99

ISBN 0-89051-250-7 • 80 pages • 8-1/2 x 11 • Casebound
Four-color interior

Available at Christian bookstores nationwide
Find other great titles at www.masterbooks.net